C

by
FATHER JOHN REDFORD

A Universe Publication

CONTENTS

Preface to 2009 edition

I am delighted and honoured that Joe Kelly, Editor of The Universe Catholic weekly, wishes to reprint Catholic Basics. A decade has passed since the first edition, and time has made at least my portrait out of date. Perhaps it is better to leave it in its 1990s version, as a happy memory!

Nothing is perfect and, as I have read the text through again, there is much I could put better. That will always be the case. But a full revision would in effect be a re-writing of Catholic Basics, time for which task would be difficult to find in my busy life here at Maryvale. I do think in all humility that the text as it stands is worth a second run. I have therefore made only minor adjustments to the text, adding for instance the Mysteries of Light added by Pope John Paul II of happy memory to the Rosary devotion.

I do hope in particular that it will be useful to catechists as well as to general readers that I have printed out selected texts from the Bible, the Catechism of the Catholic Church, and the documents of the Second Vatican Council where relevant in my question and answer format. I have attempted to put over not only my own thoughts, but the thoughts of the divinely inspired Sacred Scriptures, and the documents of the Catholic Church the "pillar and the ground of truth". (1 Timothy 3:15)

Perhaps my greatest hope, however, is that it will also be read by people young or not so young who will be reading about the Catholic faith perhaps for the first time. Give it a chance! God bless you.

Maryvale Institute, Birmingham, July 2009

THIS LITTLE BOOK

Catholic Basics first appeared as a series of 12 articles in *The Universe*, the most popular weekly religious newspaper in Britain. The articles appeared successively, week by week, starting just after Easter 1998.

I have shortened the text almost by half, and set it in the form of a series of Questions and Answers, in order to make *Catholic Basics* hopefully more readable in a single small volume, and indeed more economical to purchase.

Since the Second Vatican Council, which met in 1961, successive Popes have emphasised more and more the need for adult education in the Church.

This new emphasis culminated in the publication of the *Catechism of the Catholic Church* by Pope John Paul II in 1992, and in the *General Directory for Catechesis* which was published by the Vatican in 1997.

Catholics often have seen catechesis as mainly for children. No-one would deny the vital need for the formation of our children in the faith and life of the Church.

But a number of reasons have driven the Church to focus particularly on adults, who then will be able more effectively to catechise their children, being themselves more confident of their faith.

The enormous impact of secularism, the fact that two or three generations since the Second Vatican Council seem clearly to be badly formed in the knowledge of their faith, and above all the need to evangelise our unChurched, have been three of the main reasons for such a shift in emphasis.

Finally, the recent phenomenal success of the Alpha programme, which has up to now had its main success in the Anglican and Free Churches in England, has drawn attention to the need for such evangelisation to be effective and challenging to the heart as well as to the mind. *Catholic Basics*, therefore, can be used as a follow-up to an Alpha course, or perhaps as a means of evangelisation itself in a Catholic context. It could also be used at the beginning of a course in the Rite of Christian Initiation of Adults (RCIA).

It is also hoped that *Catholic Basics* will be interesting to read for anyone, whether a member of a group or not. For those who wish to pursue matters further, it will be useful to have to hand a Bible, a copy of the Catechism of the Catholic Church, and, if possible, a copy of the documents of Vatican II. Certainly, those leading a group and using *Catholic Basics* will need these volumes for reference.

But, for those who have not such hefty volumes, or who are in a situation where such volumes are not available, it is hoped that *Catholic Basics* will stand alone as a short introduction to the Catholic Faith for adults.

For that very reason, I have taken care throughout to quote in full important texts from Scripture, from the Catechism, and from various Church documents. In addition to the twelve main chapters of *Catholic Basics*, an appendix of prayers has been added. No-one who is interested in Catholicism can fail to see the supreme importance of learning to pray, learning from the example of Jesus himself who taught his disciples to pray.

This is by no means my own first excursion into the field of providing written resources for Catholic adult education. In the seventies, I wrote *We Believe* as a series of articles on the Creed in the *Catholic Gazette*, then *What Catholics Believe*, now re-published as a Catholic Classic by the Catholic Truth Society.

Finally, *Faith Alive* was a great success in the eighties, both as a series in *The Universe* and as a book published by Hodder and Stoughton. Every comedian has to renew his act; and I have found that re-writing the truths of the faith yet again in the new situation of the 1990s has itself helped to renew my own faith and Christian life. I only hope that others will find the same stimulus to continuous conversion and holiness as I find again and again from the Scriptures and from the tradition and teaching of the Catholic Church.

I am very grateful to the Principal Catholic Chaplain of the Army, the Rt. Rev. Mgr. Kevin Vasey, OBE, who requested the book initially, as a resource for his chaplains. I am also appreciative of the criticisms and suggestions of Fr Michael Masterson OBE, Senior Catholic Chaplain at HQ 3

(UK) Division, who worked very much with me on this project, together with Fr Nick Gosnell of the Army Training Regiment, Pirbright.

I do hope and pray that this little book will help many in the Army to renew their faith and spiritual life. Most helpful also were the suggestions of my friend Fr Alexander Brown, Parish Priest of Hednesford, Staffs.

Finally, my thanks are especially due to Joe Kelly, the Editor of *The Universe*, who has encouraged this project from the beginning.

I thank the Medjugorje Society for giving me a free trip to that centre in Croatia linked with claimed apparitions of Mary, the mother of Jesus. It was during this trip, in August 1998, that I finished *Catholic Basics*.

The Church at this point has not pronounced on the authenticity of the visions at Medjugorje. But the thousands of people of all ages, especially young people, who gather to pray at the Blessed Sacrament, to go to Mass, to go to Confession, and manifest their faith, are sure indications of the vitality of the Catholic faith today, and of the power of the prayers of the Mother of God.

We see her not as a goddess, but as our very human spiritual mother. May all who read this booklet know the love of the mother of us all now in heaven, and come to faith in her divine Son.

Father John Redford, Maryvale Institute
Birmingham, November 1998

CATHOLIC
BASICS

by

FATHER JOHN REDFORD

CHAPTER I
THE PURPOSE OF LIFE

Q. Am I just a piece of meat? Is life meaningless? Am I just destined for the scrap-heap, like my car or washing machine? Am I just a chance mixture of bacteria and bones, thrown together by a mindless evolution?

A. NO! The Catechism of the Catholic Church teaches that our life has a purpose; to find true happiness in God our loving Creator.

> *27 The desire for God is written in the human heart, because man* is created by God and for God; and God never ceases to draw man to himself. Only in God will he find the truth and happiness he never stops searching for:*
>
> *The dignity of man rests above all on the fact that he is called to communion with God. This invitation to converse with God is addressed to man as soon as he comes into being. For if man exists it is because God has created him through love, and through love continues to hold him in existence. He cannot live fully according to truth unless he freely acknowledges that love and entrusts himself to his creator.*

Q. But cannot we find happiness in the ordinary things of life; in human relationships, in a good meal, in football, in music, in a job well done?

A. Yes, of course. God has made us material beings, and he wants us to be happy on this earth. But there is a spiritual side to our being, which can only be satisfied with God. As Augustine said, 'You have made us for yourself, Lord, and our hearts are restless until they find their rest in you':-

> With the human person's openness to truth and beauty, his sense of moral goodness, his freedom and the voice of his conscience, with his longings for the infinite and for happiness, man questions himself about God's existence. In all this he discerns signs of his spiritual soul. The soul, the "seed of eternity we bear in ourselves, irreducible to the merely material," can have its origin only in God. (CCC 33)

Q. But does not all this end in death?

A. Certainly not. The fact that we have an immortal soul means that death is not the end. This conquers the terrible fear we all have of extinction.

> It is in regard to death that man's condition is most shrouded in doubt. Man is tormented not only by pain and by the gradual breaking-up of his body but also, and even more, by the dread of forever ceasing to be.
> But a deep instinct leads him rightly to shrink from and to reject the utter ruin and total loss of his personality. Because he bears in himself the seed of eternity, which cannot be reduced to mere matter, he rebels against death.
> All the aids made available by technology, however useful they may be, cannot set his anguished mind at rest. They may prolong his life-span; but this does not satisfy his heartfelt longing, one that can never be stifled, for a life to come. (GS 18)

Q. But how do we know that our end will be eternal happiness?

A. Because the Son of God, Jesus Christ (we will be speaking of him much more later!) said to a violent thief hanging on the cross beside him "I promise you, today you will be with me in paradise." *(Luke 23:43)*
That was because the robber had asked Jesus 'remember me when you come into your kingdom'. Jesus said he certainly would!
Anyone who is truly sorry for sin and asks God for forgiveness will be offered the same eternal happiness which is our final destiny as human beings. THAT IS TRUE WHATEVER WRONG WE HAVE DONE.

Q. But how do we know that God even exists? Could it not all be a religious con-job? After all, we cannot actually SEE God?

A. This is where the traditional proofs for God's existence are relevant. They amount to this; that nothing comes from nothing. The Big Bang cannot be the origin of everything. What caused the Big Bang? The old argument for God's existence by the great 13th century theologian St. Thomas Aquinas is still valid after nearly one thousand years:-

> *Everything therefore which is moved, must be moved by something else. If therefore that by which it is moved is itself moved, then it follows that that which acts as the mover is also itself moved by something else; and that again by something else.*

But here we cannot proceed to infinity; because in this case there would be no first mover, and, in consequence, neither would there be anything else moving, because secondary movements do not move unless moved by a primary mover, just as a stick does not move unless it is moved by a moving hand. Therefore it is necessary to proceed to some Prime Mover, which is itself not moved by anything; and this everyone understands as God. (Summa Theologica I.Q.2.a.3)

Q. But who made God?

A. It is no argument to say, 'Who made God?' What Aquinas is arguing to is an Unmoved Mover, or an Uncaused Cause. No one made God. God is the one uncaused cause, which is necessary for anything to exist. Nothing comes from nothing. Aquinas is arguing to a 'Prime Mover, which is not moved by anything; and this everyone understands as God'.

Note that God is not 'the old man with a beard upstairs'. God is for Aquinas a total mystery, if you like 'The Unknown X' who is the only possible explanation for everything that is.

Q. But is not 'evolution' the answer to everything?

A. No. Nothing prevents a person who believes in God also believing in evolution. There may be, and no doubt are, secondary causes working in the process of evolution, like the 'survival of the fittest'.

But why do the fittest have the power to survive? Why are they able to look after themselves? Surely, only because they are given the power to do so by something else.

Now we are back to the arguments of Aquinas again. Evolution must have an uncaused cause, which we call God.

Q. But did it not all come from chance?

A. No. Aquinas' argument from design, Argument No. 4, is relevant here. If we look at a car, we assume that there must be an intelligence to have put such a complicated piece of machinery together. But the makeup of our little finger is much more complicated than a Rolls Royce.

How can an atheist posit that the human being was thrown together by chance? How much more rational is the existence of God to explain the existence of all things?

Q. But how do I begin this relationship with my Creator, in whom is my final happiness?

A. Easy. Learn to say the 'Our Father', the prayer which Jesus himself taught his disciples to say (look at Matthew's Gospel 6:9-13):

Our Father who art in heaven,
We address God as Father, because he is our loving creator. We say 'who art in heaven' because he dwells everywhere but also above everywhere.

Hallowed be thy name.
We always keep the name of God sacred, and give God the worship and infinite respect due to him.

Thy kingdom come. Thy will be done, On earth as it is in heaven.

We unite ourselves with the will of God in everything we do; as Jesus said just before his arrest, *(Matthew 26:42)*.

Give us this day our daily bread;

We pray that all our needs, material and spiritual, will be met day by day; but not ours as individuals alone, but the needs of all people. Not simply 'my daily bread' but 'our daily bread'!

And forgive us our trespasses, As we also have forgiven those who trespass against us

We ask for God's forgiveness for our sins; and promise that we will be generous in forgiving others their sins against us.

And lead us not into temptation, But deliver us from evil. Amen.

We pray that God will not allow us to fall into temptation, but will give us the grace to resist temptation to do evil.

GREAT CHRISTIANS
ST. IGNATIUS LOYOLA

Ignatius was a Spanish nobleman, who had a relish for war. He was brave, and ambitious for his family. But, fighting a battle, he was wounded, and had several months convalescence.

While lying on his bed of sickness, he borrowed a copy of the Gospels, and his life was transformed.

He became as brave a soldier for Christ as he had been previously in the army.

He lived a life of fasting and poverty, and soon gathered a group of like-minded men around him, whom he called the 'Company (called by us the 'Society') of Jesus'; the 'God Squad' if you like!

The Jesuits, for such they were called eventually, had enormous success as missionaries and teachers in the Church.

Ignatius wrote a whole way of prayer called 'The Spiritual Exercises'; spiritual basic training, in fact. We are attempting something like spiritual basic training in this booklet!

His feast is July 31.

CHAPTER 2
FOLLOWING THE RIGHT WAY

Q. Is not Catholic morality based only upon rules and regulations?

A. Not at all. It is based first and foremost upon the value of the human person as made in God's image.

Listen to the First Chapter of Genesis:-

> Then God said, "Let us make humankind in our image, according to our likeness; and let them have dominion over the fish of the sea, and over the birds of the air, and over the cattle, and over all the wild animals of the earth, and over every creeping thing that creeps upon the earth."
> So God created humankind in his image, in the image of God he created them; male and female he created them. God blessed them, and God said to them, "Be fruitful and multiply, and fill the earth and subdue it; and have dominion over the fish of the sea and over the birds of the air and over every living thing that moves upon the earth."
> God said, "See, I have given you every plant yielding seed that is upon the face of all the earth, and every tree with seed in its fruit; you shall have them for food'. (Genesis 1:26-29)

That is why the first law that God taught his people was not to kill, because to kill would be to destroy someone made in God's own image of mind and will:-

Whoever sheds the blood of a human, by a human shall that person's blood be shed; for in his own image God made humankind. And you, be fruitful and multiply, abound on the earth and multiply in it. (Genesis 9:6)

Q. But why did God allow so much killing in the Bible? Was that not against his own law?

A. The law against killing did not forbid killing in war, or killing in punishment for some serious crime. In fact, we can put it another way. Life is so sacred that it must be defended, even if you kill in defence of that life.

A better description of 'You shall not kill' in the Old Testament was 'You shall do no murder'.

The Church has continued this interpretation, justifying killing in self defence, in war, and even capital punishment.

But the killing of the innocent human being was always seen as a horrendous crime in the Old Testament and in Christian tradition; hence the fact that the Church does not permit abortion, simply because it amounts to the killing of an innocent human being, made in the image and likeness of God, even if only at this stage in the womb. Likewise the Church condemns as wrong the destruction of human embryos for experimentation. Science can surely find other means of curing disease without taking human life at its inception.

Q. Are not the Ten Commandments just a case of God wielding the big stick?:-

A. Not in any way. God called his people out of slavery in Egypt to lead them to a new land, where they would follow his way.

The Ten Commandments were not just a series of 'don'ts', but rather a declaration of human rights for the people. Those rules ensured respect for the dignity of human beings.

And the basis of that respect was first to serve the true God. If they respected God, then they would respect those made in his image:-

> *Therefore you shall keep his statutes and his commandments, which I command you this day, that it may go well with you, and with your children after you, and that you may prolong your days in the land which the LORD your God gives you for ever.* (Deuteronomy 4:40)

Q. Are not the Ten Commandments rather old-fashioned today?

A. Not at all. The Ten Commandments are an expression of the basic law of right and wrong written in human nature.

To worship God, not to steal, not to commit adultery, not to bear false witness, all these commandments are part of God's eternal plan for our life on earth. They cannot change, but our understanding of those laws does develop down the centuries.

Q. Then why do we need those commandments written down in the Bible?

A. Because we are not perfect, and sometimes manage to blur the truth of what we know to be right and wrong!

That is why the Church always teaches those Ten Commandments originally given all those years ago, and interprets them in the light of the Holy Spirit, which is always given to the Church to help us understand the truth of God's way.

Here are the Ten Commandments, the 'bare bones' of what is set out in two texts.

There are two accounts of these Commandments, one in the book of Exodus 20:2-17, the other in Deuteronomy 5:6-21.

But the Church has handed down a simple version to be learnt, summarising the longer form of the Commandments in the Old Testament. See p. 445-6, CCC, 'A Traditional Catechetical Formula':-

1. I AM THE LORD YOUR GOD.
    YOU SHALL NOT HAVE
    STRANGE GODS BEFORE ME.

2. YOU SHALL NOT TAKE THE NAME
    OF THE LORD YOUR GOD IN VAIN.

3. REMEMBER TO KEEP HOLY THE
    LORD'S DAY.

4. HONOUR YOUR FATHER AND
    YOUR MOTHER.

5. YOU SHALL NOT KILL.

6. YOU SHALL NOT COMMIT
    ADULTERY.

7. YOU SHALL NOT STEAL

8. YOU SHALL NOT BEAR FALSE
    WITNESS AGAINST YOUR
    NEIGHBOUR.

9. YOU SHALL NOT COVET YOUR
    NEIGHBOUR'S WIFE.

10. YOU SHALL NOT COVET YOUR
    NEIGHBOUR'S GOODS.

The following is an ancient Hebrew hymn contained in the Book of Psalms which you might call a Psalm of Commitment, where we reject the way of evil and choose good, God's way:-

PSALM 1
Blessed is the man who walks not in the counsel of the wicked, nor stands in the way of sinners, nor sits in the seat of scoffers; but his delight is in the law of the LORD, and on his law he meditates day and night.

He is like a tree planted by streams of water, that yields its fruit in its season, and its leaf does not wither.

In all that he does, he prospers. The wicked are not so, but are like chaff which the wind drives away.

Therefore the wicked will not stand in the judgment, nor sinners in the congregation of the righteous; for the LORD knows the way of the righteous, but the way of the wicked will perish. (Psalm 1:1-6)

AND NOW, ONE WHO DID NOT
ALWAYS CHOOSE THE RIGHT WAY;
BUT WHO ALWAYS KNEW THE WAY BACK.

KING DAVID, B.C. 1010-970.
Cf. I Samuel 16-II Samuel 24. Reads like a novel!

Christians usually honour saints who lived after the time of Christ. But a very special saint who lived a thousand years before Christ was King David.

He was anointed king by the prophet Samuel, while still a shepherd boy near Bethlehem.

When David grew up, he entered the court of King Saul, who had displeased the prophet Samuel.

Saul became more and more jealous of David, especially after David acted as champion against the Philistine enemy of the Jews, and slew the huge Philistine warrior Goliath.

David fled to become a guerilla leader, although he refused to slay the king, the 'Lord's Anointed' even when he had the chance.

Eventually, Saul was killed by the Philistines in battle, and David became king. He conquered Jerusalem, then a pagan city, and established the worship of the true God in Jerusalem.

He was faithful to God; but he also was a sinner. He saw a beautiful woman called Bathsheba bathing on top of a roof, and lusted after her.

He wanted her for his wife; so he deliberately sent Uriah the Hittite, her husband, one of his guards, to certain death in battle, in order to marry his wife Bathsheba.

The prophet Nathan denounced David, who repented of his sin, though suffered the loss of their first child.

David was called the 'Messiah', meaning 'Anointed'. He became a symbol of the hopes of Israel, particularly when they lost their kingdom and became a vassal state of a succession of empires.

The name Christ, the title of Jesus, means 'Messiah', in this case a king not of a nation, but the king of God's new kingdom comprising the whole world.

CHAPTER 3
A NEW COVENANT

Q. We have the Ten Commandments. Is that not enough to serve God? Why do we need all this paraphernalia of religion?

A. The problem is that we as a human race, and as individuals, do not obey the Ten Commandments. This was God's constant complaint against his people Israel, whom he called to follow him. The prophet Hosea (8th century B.C.) saw God's people as an unfaithful child:-

> *When Israel was a child, I loved him, and out of Egypt I called my son. The more I called them, the more they went from me; they kept sacrificing to the Ba'als, and burning incense to idols. Yet it was I who taught Ephraim to walk, I took them up in my arms; but they did not know that I healed them. (Hosea 11:1-4)*

Q. But, surely, I am not as bad as all that? I do not steal anyone's property, I do not sleep with another man's wife, I try and look after my ageing mother and father. The Israelites worshipped false gods like Baal. But I have no idols in my house!

A. That may well be true. But a little self examination might reveal some problems. For instance, do we consider the neglect of religion to be a sin?
It clearly is in view of the Ten Commandments, the command to worship the Lord your God. People say 'I am not religious' as if to be religious were some kind of nut!

The Second Vatican Council's Constitution on the Church in the Modern World, *Gaudium et Spes*, puts its finger on the button:-

> *In the past it was the exception to repudiate God and religion to the point of abandoning them, and then only in individual cases; but nowadays it seems a matter of course to reject them as incompatible with scientific progress and a new kind of humanism.* (No. 7)

Q. We are not going to talk about sin, now, are we?

A. Unfortunately, yes! It is a reality of life which must be faced. The word 'Gospel' comes from the Anglo-Saxon God spell, 'Good News'. But the Gospel is bad news before it is Good News. A person going to the doctor wants to hear the truth, that he or she is sick, and why. That is usually bad news.

The good news that the patient then wants to hear is that there is a cure. The Scriptures tell us that we are as a human race sick with a disease called sin. *(Romans 3:23)* That is the bad news. The Scriptures tell us that there is only one cure for that disease, Jesus Christ our Lord *(1 John 2:1)*. That is the good news.

If we look deeply into our lives in the light of the Ten Commandments, we find that we are not as good as perhaps we think we are.

Not only do we find ourselves doing wrong, or, even more frequently, not doing right. With St. Paul, one of the greatest Christians of all time, we find in ourselves the TENDENCY to sin. This is what Paul says:-

For I know that nothing good dwells within me, that is, in my flesh. I can will what is right, but I cannot do it. For I do not do the good I want, but the evil I do not want is what I do. Now if I do what I do not want, it is no longer I that do it, but sin which dwells within me.
So I find it to be a law that when I want to do right, evil lies close at hand. For I delight in the law of God, in my inmost self, but I see in my members another law at war with the law of my mind and making me captive to the law of sin which dwells in my members. Wretched man that I am! Who will deliver me from this body of death? (Romans 7:18-24)

Here is a committed Christian speaking after years of dedicated service in the Church. Paul is drawing attention to a sickness universal in human nature; sin. In this case, not just individual acts of sin, but A TENDENCY TOWARDS SIN, a bias in that direction.

We can recognise it in feelings of lust, greed, uncontrolled anger, selfishness, pride.

Q. What is the cause of this bias towards sin?

A. The word is 'Original Sin'. We must not misunderstand this. 'Original Sin' is a technical word in Christian thought meaning that sin which was there from the beginning (Latin *ab origine*) of the human race.

Everyone knows the story of the Fall of Adam and Eve in Genesis chapter 3; of how the Serpent tempted Eve to eat the fruit, and of how Adam followed suit. The Catechism says:-

The account of the fall in Genesis 3 uses figurative language, but affirms a primeval event, a deed that took place at the beginning of the history of man. Revelation gives us the certainty of faith that the whole of human history is marked by the original fault freely committed by our first parents. (CCC 390)

Q. What, then, WAS the 'Original Sin'?

A. We do not know, except that it was disobedience of God. 'Eating the fruit of the knowledge of good and evil' is figurative, a story. What we do know is that, as a result of this disobedience, the first man and woman lost that relationship with God which was there from the beginning. This relationship had then to be restored.

Q. How, then, did we all 'catch the disease' of Original Sin?

A. This original sin, the Catechism goes on to say, is not a personal fault of ours as individuals, but does explain the tendency to sin which we all experience:-

Although it is proper to each individual, original sin does not have the character of a personal fault in any of Adam's descendants. It is a deprivation of original holiness and justice, but human nature has not been totally corrupted: it is wounded in the natural powers proper to it, subject to ignorance, suffering and the dominion of death, and inclined to sin - an inclination to evil that is called "concupiscence." (CCC 405)

Q. But I thought that science has disproved Adam and Eve. Did we not all come from apes?

A. Pope Pius XII, the Pope during and just after the Second World War, made it clear that Catholics could hold that our BODIES could have evolved from the lower animals. But the Church insists that at some stage in the evolutionary process, God implanted a human soul in the first human beings. It was those first human beings, our 'first parents', who were responsible for the first sin, the Original Sin, which was transmitted down the human chain.

Q. But how can 'sin' be transmitted?

A. That is a mystery, to which we do not have the complete answer. But, in these days of genes and transmitted characteristics from parent to child (e.g. DNA), the idea of a transmitted FAULT, a tendency towards sin, is no longer completely far fetched. If traits of our personality can be hereditary, why not the two elements of Original Sin, the loss of a relationship with God plus the tendency towards sin be also hereditary?

Q. Is that not all very unfair, that the rest of us should suffer from the sin of our first parents thousands of years ago?

A. In principle, it is no more unfair than an infant receiving from its parents a transmitted disease which gives that child a huge disadvantage in life. Our actions have consequences not only for ourselves, but for our children and those dependent on us. God allows us to be responsible, even for the consequences of our errors. But - and this is the Good News - with the disease comes the cure. As the prophet Jeremiah stated, this cure, was the New Covenant:-

> *"Behold, the days are coming, says the LORD, when I will make a new covenant with the house of Israel and the house of Judah, not like the covenant which I made with their fathers when I took them by the hand to bring them out of the land of Egypt, my covenant which they broke, though I was their husband, says the LORD. But this is the covenant which I will make with the house of Israel after those days, says the LORD: I will put my law within them, and I will write it upon their hearts; and I will be their God, and they shall be my people. And no longer shall each man teach his neighbour and each his brother, saying, 'Know the LORD,' for they shall all know me, from the least of them to the greatest, says the LORD; for I will forgive their iniquity, and I will remember their sin no more."*
> (Jeremiah 31:31)

God promised Jeremiah (c.610 B.C.) hundreds of years before Christ that in the future, God's law would not just be written on tablets of stone, like the Ten Commandments. That law would be written on people's hearts, so that they would WANT to do what God wanted. That Law would be lived by Jesus Christ, and communicated to our hearts through his Spirit.

This is the saint whom many people feel is more like Christ than anyone. The law of God was most certainly written on his heart!

The Italians simply call him *Il Santo* ('The Saint'). Born the son of a wealthy merchant, Francis joined the family business.

Returning from a business trip, his father was not too pleased to find that his son had stripped himself naked in the public square and put on an old sack. Francis had then embraced a beggar, seeing Christ in him.

Francis soon gathered a group to follow Christ in complete poverty. This group expanded to become the great Franciscan Order, which by its preaching and living the life of Christ has brought so many people to become themselves disciples of Christ.

When St. Francis went to Israel, where the Moslems and Christians were fighting each other, the Moslem ruler of that land had so much respect for St. Francis as a holy man that he gave him full protection.

Not only Christians, but people of other religions, recognised the law of Christ written in his heart.

His feast is October 4.

CHAPTER 4
JESUS THE WAY

Let us sum up so far.

1. We as human beings are made in God's image and likeness. Our reason is able to know of God's existence, and is able to communicate with God because of our spiritual nature (our 'soul').

2. We are able to know something about the moral law from our reason, from our nature as human beings, what is right and wrong. God has helped us in this by revealing to us the Ten Commandments.

3. But we have a tendency to sin, which means that, while we know what is right, we often do not do it. This tendency to sin is both as individuals and as a community, as the Old Testament prophets tell us.

Q. How does Jesus solve the problem?

A. Jesus shows us the Way to God when we become his disciples. He is not only our divine Master. He is our friend.

Q. What does it mean to become his disciples?

A. Firstly if we have committed sins against the Ten Commandments, we must be sorry for our sins, and promise to follow God's law. To the woman who had committed adultery, Jesus said, "I do not condemn you". But then he said, "Go and sin no more" *(John 8:11)*. And Zacchaeus, the nasty little cheat of a tax collector, who had extorted money ('You shall not steal') promised "If I have cheated anybody I will pay him back four times the amount" *(Luke 19:8)*.

Secondly, even if people have not disobeyed the Ten Commandments, Jesus still wants them to follow him to gain 'eternal life', which we cannot obtain for ourselves, no matter how good we are:-

> *A man came up to Jesus, saying, "Teacher, what good deed must I do, to have eternal life?" And he said to him, "Why do you ask me about what is good? One there is who is good. If you would enter life, keep the commandments."*
>
> *He said to him, "Which?" And Jesus said, "You shall not kill, You shall not commit adultery, You shall not steal, You shall not bear false witness, Honour your father and mother, and, You shall love your neighbour as yourself."*
>
> *The young man said to him, "All these I have observed; what do I still lack?" Jesus said to him, "If you would be perfect, go, sell what you possess and give to the poor, and you will have treasure in heaven; and come, follow me."*
>
> *When the young man heard this he went away sorrowful; for he had great possessions. And Jesus said to his disciples, "Truly, I say to you, it will be hard for a rich man to enter the kingdom of heaven. (Matthew 19:16-23)*

Q. But does that mean we have to leave everything and give away all our material possessions?

A. Not usually. It did for the rich young ruler, because Jesus saw that riches were a barrier to his happiness with God. But for the man who had been cured of his terrible madness, the 'legion of devils',

Jesus would not let him leave his home town, but said 'Go home to your people and tell them all that the Lord in his mercy has done for you' *(Luke 5:19)*. What matters is that we follow Jesus in the way he wants us to do. That is what the rich young ruler was unable to do.

Q. But why follow Jesus?

A. Because he is truly the Son of God, come to earth to save us.

Q. How do we know this?

A. First, by his manner of birth.

- The Gospels of Matthew and Luke state that Jesus was born of a young woman called Mary, and was conceived without intercourse with a man. *(Matthew 1:18-23, Luke 1:26-38)*.
- The virginal conception of Jesus was from the beginning the object of ridicule by those who did not accept the Christian faith. There was even a story among the Romans in the Second Century that what really happened was something rather different, and much more mundane.
  A soldier went into Mary pretending that he was an angel; and the child Jesus was born in an all too natural way!
- But the early Christians remained firm in their faith in the miraculous conception of Jesus by the power of the Holy Spirit. And all modern attempts to explain the virginal conception for instance using parallels from pagan myths have foundered. Virginal conception, after all, is hardly a difficult miracle for the Creator to perform!

- The virginal conception of Jesus is first and foremost a sign that Jesus is the Son of God. He constantly called God his Father, even when only a small boy of twelve *(Luke 2:49)*.
- The early Fathers of the Church saw the virginal conception as a new beginning, needed because of the bad start we had with Adam and Eve. Ordinary human sexual intercourse was handing down Original Sin.

  Now, with Mary's act of faith as opposed to Eve's submitting to temptation, we have a new start of fidelity to God. (It does not mean of course that sex in itself is a wrong or bad thing!).
- Mary's act of faith is also the reason for Catholic devotion to Mary. Mary was truly human like the rest of us, but was preserved free from sin (the Immaculate Conception) to be a worthy 'God-bearer' (theotokos, Mother of God).

Q. But how did Jesus himself show us who he really was?

A. He showed who he was *'by the total fact of his presence and self-manifestation-by words and works, signs and miracles, but above all by his death and glorious resurrection, and finally by sending the Spirit of truth'*. (Dei Verbum, No. 4). We often say that 'Jesus died for us'. But, as the Second Vatican Council tells us, he also lived for us. Everything he did, he did as God become man; and everything he did, he did for you and me.

Q. What good was his terrible death on the Cross for us?

A. Because he offered the perfect act of worship to the Father, his own life for us. The Old Testament had an elaborate sacrificial ritual. But the prophets tell us that sacrifices are useless wihout a pure heart.

> With what shall I come before the LORD, and bow myself before God on high? Shall I come before him with burnt offerings, with calves a year old? Will the LORD be pleased with thousands of rams, with ten thousands of rivers of oil? Shall I give my first-born for my transgression, the fruit of my body for the sin of my soul? He has showed you, O man, what is good; and what does the LORD require of you but to do justice, and to love kindness, and to walk humbly with your God? (Micah 6:6-8).

The Psalmist gives us the same sentiments. God wants us, he wants our praise and our confession of faith. He does not want our sacrifices, as the psalmist says to God in his prayer. (Psalm 40:6-8):-

> Sacrifice and offering you do not desire; but you have given me an open ear. Burnt offering and sin offering you have not required. Then I said, "Lo, I come; in the roll of the book it is written of me; I delight to do thy will, O my God; thy law is within my heart."

But who would come to God with a pure heart to offer that perfect sacrifice of his life? Only Jesus. The great theologian Anselm of Canterbury (1033-1109) argued that God required an infinite sacrifice to satisfy an infinite indignity which God had suffered through the sin of the human race.

Only one was able to offer that infinite sacrifice, one who was not only human by nature but also divine, Jesus Christ. When he said while hanging on the Cross, 'Father, forgive them, they do not know what they are doing' *(Luke 23:34)* he was referring to us as well as to those who actually crucified him then.

Q. But does not this make God the Father vindictive, wanting his 'pound of flesh', the life of his innocent son for us sinners?

A. No. God could have saved the world simply by saying from heaven "I forgive". But, for us humans, we need to know the cost of sin, how horrible it is, causing the death of his Son. The cross is a judgement on sin. *(John 16:8)*. At the same time, we need to know that the Cross is our way to God, taking up our cross to follow Christ. Like Christ, we die to sin in order to live to God. The Christian life is not an easy touch, but a tough pathway to life. Christ is our example. This is all part of the Plan.

Q. Why, then, is the Resurrection of Christ the centre of our faith?

A. The Resurrection is the centre of our faith because it sums up everything Jesus came to do for us. Athanasius, (296-373), the famous Church Father, said that in Jesus Christ, 'God became man in order that man should become divine'.
The prize is eternity with God. Jesus Christ did not only come to earth to die and forgive us our sins. More than that, he came to give us a share in the life of God, through giving us his Spirit:-

As Christ was raised from the dead by the glory of the Father, we too might walk in newness of life. For if we have been united with him in a death like his, we shall certainly be united with him in a resurrection like his (Romans 6:5-6)

Q. How do we know that Jesus actually rose from the dead? How do we know that it was not a con-job?

A. The Gospels insist that the tomb was found empty that first Easter morning, and that Jesus appeared to his amazed disciples as risen from the dead. *(Matthew 28, Mark 16, Luke 24, John 20-21).* The Catechism for its part insists that the accounts of the Resurrection are not myth, but history. *(CCC 639-647)* Christ rose body and soul to be with his heavenly Father.

The Resurrection means:-

*   That Jesus showed finally that he was the Incarnate Son of God, because death could not hold him. While on earth, Jesus showed himself as transfigured, recalling that glory which is none other than God himself *(Matthew 17:1-8).* But finally, he appears to his disciples in the full glory of his risen body. Doubting Thomas says, no longer doubting, 'My Lord and My God' *(John 20:28).*

*   That Jesus broke through the veil of his flesh to arrive at the heavenly sanctuary, with God his Father. He now offers perfect worship for us eternally, and we can join in with that worship here below. *(See Hebrews 9:11-14).*

Catholics, and incidentally Orthodox Christians and some Christians of the Reformation tradition too, have a great devotion to Mary. We do not see her as a goddess, but as a human being like ourselves, who said "Yes" to God when the angel came to her at the Annunciation. We believe that she shared in the life of Christ in a special way as his mother. She shared in the joy of his birth, in the success of his ministry, and then in the sorrows of his death. It is Catholic faith that she shared in his sinlessness, through being Immaculately Conceived, i.e. conceived without sin. And at the end of her life on earth, she shared in his Resurrection by not waiting until the final resurrection of the dead for body and soul to be joined, as we must (i.e. the Assumption).

One of the most popular Catholic prayers is the Hail Mary:-

> Hail, Mary, full of grace, the Lord is with thee. Blessed art thou among women, and blessed is the fruit of thy womb, Jesus. Holy Mary, Mother of God, pray for us sinners, now and at the hour of our death. Amen.

Mary has many feasts including January 1, the Feast of Mary Mother of God.

CHAPTER 5
ME, A MEMBER OF THE CHURCH?

Q. Why do we need a Church? Cannot we follow Christ individually?

A. Christ himself intended that his first disciples, the Twelve, who came to be called 'apostles', should form a Church (the word means 'assembly') to spread his message and the new spiritual life he brings.

> Now the eleven disciples went to Galilee, to the mountain to which Jesus had directed them. When they saw him, they worshiped him; but some doubted. And Jesus came and said to them, "All authority in heaven and on earth has been given to me. Go therefore and make disciples of all nations, baptizing them in the name of the Father and of the Son and of the Holy Spirit, and teaching them to obey everything that I have commanded you. And remember, I am with you always, to the end of the age. (Matthew 28:16-20).

Q. Why did Christ ascend into heaven? Could not he himself have stayed behind here on earth to lead the Church?

A. The Ascension is not a primitive space probe. It is the return of Jesus to the state he was before, namely as God.
This state, as we have seen, is essentially invisible and transcends everything. God is in everything but beyond everything. Jesus has now returned to that state.

But there is one essential difference. He has now taken his humanity with him, our humanity, in its glorified state. He is now what hopefully we shall be after the general Resurrection of the Dead at the end of time.

In his body on earth, even in his Resurrection appearances, Jesus could not be everywhere all at once. Now, having returned to his state as God with his glorified humanity, he is open to be worshipped and followed by everyone as true God and man.

Even more, his presence to us could be everywhere through his Spirit, and through the Sacraments, the signs he left to give us his life.

Q. How is Christ with us now?

A. He is with us through his Spirit, first given at the Day of Pentecost. Read Acts Chapter 2. That was the day (Pentecost means 'fifty', i.e. fifty days after Easter) when the Holy Spirit came down upon the Apostles in the form of tongues of fire. As Jesus himself said: The Holy Spirit is called the Advocate' because he helps us in our weakness.

Especially when we find it difficult to pray, or are in some special kind of difficulty, the Spirit of God is in us to help us:-

> Likewise the Spirit helps us in our weakness; for we do not know how to pray as we ought, but the Spirit himself intercedes for us with sighs too deep for words.
> And he who searches the hearts of men knows what is the mind of the Spirit, because the Spirit intercedes for the saints according to the will of God. (Rom 8:26-27)

Q. How do we become members of the Church?

A. Through Baptism, as Christ commanded before he went up to heaven. From the beginning, Christians obeyed Christ's command to baptise all nations in the name of the Father, and of the Son, and of the Holy Spirit. Baptism does not only initiate us into the society of the Church. It initiates us into the Society of God.

The most distinctive Christian doctrine is that the One God is Three Persons, Father, Son and Holy Spirit. Not three gods (three infinities, mathematicians tell us, do not make more than one if you add them up!); but God, God's Word or Idea, and God's Spirit. Baptism makes us a part of that Trinitarian life of God. We are to become adopted sons and daughters of God:-

> God's will was that men should have access to the Father, through Christ the Word made flesh, in the Holy Spirit, and thus become sharers in the divine nature. (Cf. Ephesians 2:18, 2 Peter 1:4). Dei Verbum, No. 2

Q. But how can I make sense of this 'Trinity'?

A. With difficulty! We believe that God is One. He must be because he is infinite. But God, being infinite Mind, has a Word, an image of himself, which is no less than himself. God also has a Spirit, if you like God's heart, which is the love between the Father and the Word.

These three are One, because three absolute infinities must be one, equally God but distinct from each other. In baptism, we are taken up into this life of God. We celebrate the fact that we are even now part of the life of the Trinity through Baptism, every time we make the Sign of the Cross.

Q. But who are members of this Church? Are people who are not baptised destined for hell?

A. Especially regarding eternal life with God, the Church has stated clearly that not only Christians go to heaven! The Second Vatican Council's Constitution on the Church in the Modern World states:

> For since Christ died for all, and since all are in fact called to one and the same destiny, which is divine, we must hold that the Holy Spirit offers to all the possibility of being made partners, in a way known to God, in the paschal mystery (i.e. the death and resurrection of Christ). (Gaudium et Spes, No. 24)

According to the Council, his offer refers to 'all people of good will in whose hearts grace is active invisibly'. That will include Moslems, Jews, Buddhists, Hindus, atheists and agnostics; and even those who do not know what to call themselves! These, therefore, can be given means of grace by God to get to heaven about which we know nothing. The Catholic Church has a very 'open door' policy when it comes to eternal life!

Q. What about those of other denominations, but who are baptised?

A. Regarding Christians of other denominations such as Church of England, Methodists, etc, they are in a much closer relationship to the Catholic Church. The Second Vatican Council stated that they are in some sense members of the Church by virtue of their baptism. The Decree on Ecumenism of Vatican II states:

> All who have been justified by faith in baptism are incorporated into Christ; they therefore have a right to be called Christians, and with good reason are accepted as brothers and sisters by children of the Catholic Church. (UR No. 3)

That is why it is the policy of the Catholic Church not to baptise those already baptised in other Christian denominations.

Q. Why then take the trouble to become a Catholic, if we can be saved in so many other denominations and faiths?

A. The answer to that appears arrogant, but is nevertheless true. A Catholic priest was having a discussion with a minister from another denomination. "Ah", said the minister at one point, "There are many ways to God". "That is true", replied the priest, 'But we are going HIS way'. That is the most certain way, and contains all the means of salvation. As the Second Vatican Council's decree on Ecumenism states:-

> For it is through Christ's Catholic Church alone, which is the universal help to salvation, that the fullness of the means of salvation can be obtained (Decree on Ecumenism, Unitatis Redintegratio, No. 3)

We respect other denominations and other faiths. We work with them towards unity. We celebrate what we have in common. But we believe that at the day of Pentecost, the Catholic Church was founded by Christ through the gift of the Holy Spirit. If you like, the full package of salvation was given to the Catholic Church alone. A person who realises this, and believes it, would be plain foolish to take any other pathway than the one provided by Jesus himself who is the Way, the Truth, and the Life. (John 14:6). It would be refusing to follow the truth as we see it.

It is like being told the way to your friend's home by that friend himself or herself. "Take the M1, and leave it at junction 14. Then..." You have precise instructions. But then you think, "Well, it might be nicer to take another way". So you go through the highways and byways, and get lost. Your friend would be justifiably upset if you arrived late because of such a silly decision to go your own way, when a perfect way has already been provided by the one who knows absolutely.

Q. How do I Qualify for Baptism?

A. By professing the Christian faith, and being prepared to follow the way of life of the Church left to us by Christ and the apostles. Where an adult is concerned, there must be a full commitment of personal faith. This usually implies a period of instruction. If you have a past, you can put it behind you!
For those already baptised, they are prepared for full communion with the Catholic Church.

GREAT CHRISTIANS
ST. STEPHEN

The first Christian martyr. A Jewish convert who spoke Greek, and chosen to be one of the first deacons. (Acts 6:1-7)

Stephen was in charge of distribution to the poor from Church funds.

His preaching was fearless, and he was arrested for preaching against the Temple; although he himself denied that.

The dying words of St. Stephen were words not of vengence but of love for his killers: "Lord, do not hold this sin against them" *(Acts 7:60)*.

He was stoned to death, and one of those standing by holding the coats of those stoning was a man called Paul of Tarsus, eventually to become a most famous Christian himself, St. Paul. See Acts 7:55-8:1.

St. Stephen is Patron Saint of Deacons, and of Altar Servers.

His feast is December 26.

CHAPTER 6
THE TEACHING AUTHORITY
OF THE CHURCH

Q. What is the 'magisterium'?

A. The 'magisterium' (Latin for "teaching office") is the teaching authority of the Church. Everyone in the Church has a duty to teach others about the faith, especially priests, teachers and parents. But the 'magisterium' consists of those specially appointed by Christ and the Holy Spirit to ensure that the revelation of Christ handed on to his apostles, is communicated faithfully throughout all generations.

Q. Who makes up the magisterium of the Church?

A. The Bishops of the Catholic Church are united as a College (a kind of Senate) with the Pope as Head, in Apostolic Succession to the twelve apostles. The Catechism puts it this way:-

When Christ instituted the Twelve, "he constituted (them) in the form of a college or permanent assembly, at the head of which he placed Peter, chosen from among them." Just as "by the Lord's institution, St. Peter and the rest of the apostles constitute a single apostolic college, so in like fashion the Roman Pontiff, Peter's successor, and the bishops, the successors of the apostles, are related with and united to one another". (880)

The Lord made Simon alone, whom he named Peter, the "rock" of his Church. He gave him the keys of his Church, and instituted him shepherd of the whole flock. "The office of binding and loosing which was given to Peter was also assigned to the college of apostles united to its head." This pastoral office of Peter and the other apostles belongs to the Church's very foundation and is continued by the bishops under the primacy of the Pope. (881)

The Catholic Church therefore differs from the Protestant denominations in saying that Christ actually appointed a leader for the whole Church (see Matthew 16:13-20). The Protestant position would be that Church leadership was not determined by Christ. The Orthodox Churches would accept with Catholics that Bishops are successors of the apostles, and would accept that Peter has some primacy of honour among all the patriarchs, but not complete authority over the Church on earth, which is the Catholic belief.

Q. Why do we need a teaching authority? Is not the Bible, and our own faith, sufficient for belief?

A. The existence of so many Christian denominations and conflicting beliefs proves that the Bible alone is not sufficient to settle matters of doctrine for the whole Church, or to hold the Church in unity. If the Church were simply a political party, it would make its decisions purely from reason. But regarding the Christian faith, we are dealing with revelation, with truths beyond our reason. Whereas we can know of God's existence and the natural law by reason, the Church teaches that our articles of faith, like the doctrine of the

Trinity and Christ being the Incarnate Son of God, are revealed, and can never be entirely proved. We can prove that these truths are not against reason. But ultimately we are driven to faith. As the First Vatican Council states:

> *This faith, which is the beginning of human salvation, the Catholic Church professes to be a supernatural virtue, by means of which, by the grace of God inspiring and assisting us, we believe to be true what he has revealed, not because we perceive its intrinsic truth by the natural light of reason, but because of the authority of God himself, who makes the revelation and can neither deceive nor be deceived. Faith, declares the Apostle, is the assurance of things hoped for, the conviction of things not seen.* (Hebrews 11:1) (Vatican II Dei Filius 1817)

If revelation is a supernatural gift, then we have only two alternatives. Either the individual believer is left with his or her own gift of the Holy Spirit, and we all believe what we believe that the Holy Spirit is saying to us individually (the extreme Protestant solution, with thousands of different denominations). Or we believe that Jesus Christ has left the Church with his Spirit, the Spirit of Truth, and the Church proposes to us infallibly what that revelation is. Through the assistance of the Holy Spirit, we then make the act of faith on the authority of God himself who reveals.

Q. But how do we know that Christ wanted the Pope, the Bishop of Rome, to be the Head of the Church on earth?

A. The Catholic Church claims that the Pope's authority stems from the fact that he is the succcessor of Peter, the big fisherman, one of the twelve apostles who was made by Jesus leader of the group. The following is the statement of the First Vatican Council, which met in Rome in 1870:

> We teach and declare that, according to the gospel evidence, a primacy of jurisdiction over the whole Church of God was immediately and directly promised to the blessed apostle Peter and conferred on him by Christ the Lord.
> It was to Simon alone, to whom he had already said, You shall be called Cephas, that the Lord, after his confession, You are the Christ, the son of the living God, spoke these words:

> Blessed are you, Simon Bar-Jona. For flesh and blood has not revealed this to you, but my Father who is in heaven. And I tell you, you are Peter, and on this rock I will build my Church, and the gates of the underworld shall not prevail against it. I will give you the keys of the kingdom of heaven, and whatever you bind on earth shall be bound in heaven, and whatever you loose one earth shall be loosed in heaven.
> (Matthew 16:17-19)

Q. But surely the Church cannot seriously claim that the Pope, a human being, is infallible?

A. Only when he speaks as Head of the Church on earth in matters of faith.
Note carefully what Vatican I says about the Pope's infallibility. The language is very precise:-

> *We teach and define as a divinely revealed dogma that when the Roman pontiff speaks ex cathedra, that is, when, in the exercise of his office as shepherd and teacher of all Christians, in virtue of his supreme apostolic authority, he defines a doctrine concerning faith or morals to be held by the whole Church, he possesses, by the divine assistance promised to him in blessed Peter, that infallibility which the divine Redeemer willed his Church to enjoy in defining doctrine concerning faith or morals.*

The Pope, then, is not infallible when he talks about the weather! In fact, there have only been two infallible papal definitions in recent centuries. when he defined the Immaculate Conception of Mary in 1868, and in defining the Assumption of the Virgin Mary in 1951.

But the most important aspect of the definition of papal infallibility is its underpinning of the infallible teaching authority of the whole Church.

The usual way in which doctrine is defined is the Pope together with the Apostolic College of Bishops.

There have been twenty-one Ecumenical Councils in the history of the Church, on average about one per century.

They have been momentous, settling thorny issues in matters of doctrine; like the Council of Nicea 325 defining Christ as 'of one being (homoousios) with the Father'; and Trent defining that Christ left seven sacraments, as opposed to those Christians who said that there were only two, Baptism and the Eucharist.

The Sacraments taught by the Catholic Church as left by Christ for us are:
Baptism, Confirmation, Holy Eucharist, Penance, Sacrament of Anointing of the Sick, Holy Orders, Marriage.

To understand the teaching authority of the Catholic Church is most important. It is the most criticised aspect of Catholic life.

And it is necessary for a Catholic to trust the teaching authority of the Church, fulfilling Christ's promise that: "When the Spirit of truth comes, he will guide you into all the truth" (John 16:13).

GREAT CHRISTIANS
ST. THOMAS MORE AND ST. JOHN FISHER

A London lawyer, Thomas More rose to be Chancellor (i.e. Prime Minister) under King Henry VIII. A great scholar, writer and humanist, friend of Erasmus of Rotterdam, the Renaissance scholar and wit. Thomas More was not prepared to petition the Pope for the annulment of the King's marriage to Queen Catherine of Aragon. Henry wanted to marry Anne Boleyn, his latest mistress.

The Pope was convinced that the marriage with Catherine was perfectly valid, and would not give way in spite of enormous political pressure from the English politicians of the day.

Henry VIII countered by declaring himself to be 'Head on Earth of the Church of England', and the terrified English bishops nearly all concurred, with the notable exception of John Fisher, Bishop of Rochester.

Both Bishop Fisher and Thomas More insisted that Christ made Peter the head of the Church on earth. While they protested their loyalty to the King as the leader of the State, they could not give him an authority over the Church which Christ had given to the Bishop of Rome as the sucessor of Peter.

Henry VIII had More and Fisher both beheaded ostensibly for treason, to the horror of the whole of Europe. They were both canonised as saints in 1935 by Pope Pius XI. St. Thomas More prayed for his enemies, on the scaffold: 'Pray for me as I will for thee, that we may merrily meet in heaven'.

They share the same feast on June 22.

RIACT...
O...
...NINFEN NIS...
...ENS...
RITA AQUAE...
...DITER...
AGRESTI LP...
YONTON quit...
H LUSER...
NTIM...

NIA NGOITOI...
OPQES EPTI...
PEL SGIRAPTA...
ANDEM...

EICTI AI TYPHON...
DEATH...
PENIEN desepera...
QEREUCIIS PERUIGIL...

CHAPTER 7
THE HOLY BIBLE

Q. Why should I read the Bible?

A. Because the Bible is the prime source of spiritual nourishment for any Christian. As the Second Vatican Council says:-

> *Just as the Church has always venerated the Body of Christ so she has always held in reverence the sacred Scriptures... In the sacred books our Father who is in heaven lovingly meets his children and speaks with them; such force and power are present in the word of God that it remains the Church's support and source of energy, and for her children a strength of the faith, a food of the soul, and a pure and never failing source of spiritual life. Hence one may admirably apply to holy Scripture the phrase: 'For the word of God is living and effectual', Heb 4:12 which 'is able to build up and to give inheritance among all the sanctified'. (Acts 20:32; cf. I Thess 2:13) DV 21*

Q. But HOW should I read the Bible?

A. We should read the Bible expecting to be led daily closer to Christ our Lord. This happened to a court official in the story in the Acts of the Apostles. The Christian deacon Philip saw him reading the Scriptures sitting in his chariot:-

He asked, "Do you understand what you are reading?" He replied, "How can I, unless someone guides me?" And he invited Philip to get in and sit beside him... Then Philip began to speak, and starting with this Scripture, he proclaimed to him the good news about Jesus. As they were going along the road, they came to some water; and the court official said, "Look, here is water! What is to prevent me from being baptized?" He commanded the chariot to stop, and both of them, Philip and the eunuch, went down into the water, and Philip baptized him. When they came up out of the water, the Spirit of the Lord snatched Philip away; the eunuch saw him no more, and went on his way rejoicing. (Acts 8:26-39)

Q. But the Bible is a long book, and is sometimes very obscure. How can we understand it?

A. The Bible took more than a thousand years to write, from the earliest traditions of the Old Testament c.1000 B.C. until the last New Testament book was written at the end of the first century A.D. The Bible contains history, legal sections, stories, even novels (Ruth, Tobit), prophetic visions, poetry, hymns.

All the books of the Bible cannot all be interpreted in the same way. The Bible is a coat of many colours. It is the Word of God. But it was written by human beings: and we have to understand what the human author has to say in order to understand what God wants to say to us. Vatican II teaches:-

Seeing that in holy Scripture God has spoken by human beings, and in a human manner, the interpreter of holy Scripture in order to perceive what God willed to communicate to us, should investigate what the sacred writers really intended to signify and God was pleased to manifest by their words.

To discover the sacred writer's purpose one should pay attention, among other matters, to the literary forms of expression. Truth is, in effect, set forth and enunciated in a diversity of fashions, in texts that are, in varying ways historical or prophetic or poetic, or that employ other modes of expression.

It is right for the interpreter to discover the sense which a sacred writer intended to express and did express, in certain definite circumstances, according to the conditions of his time and of his culture, and according to the classes of literature then in use. (DV 12)

Q. But is the Bible not sometimes myth? Like the Creation story, telling us that the world was created in six days, when modern science tells us that it took millions of years to create?

A. God does not only speak to us in the form of strict history. He speaks 'in a diversity of fashions'. There is no conflict between the six days of creation in Genesis Chapter 1 as compared with modern scientific cosmology saying that the world took millions of years to create. The 'six days' are symbolic of a week's work, and the end of which God, like every good member of the human race, has a day of rest! That is picture language.

It is not a scientific description. The point of the story of Creation in its historical context is to point out that God created all the world, and created it all good. The Creation story contradicted ancient mythologies which said that the gods created the world as part of an unholy war between them!

Q. But how do we know that the Bible is not all myth?

A. By trusting the Church's interpretation of Scripture, and the expert scholars who guide us in our reading of the Bible. For instance, the Church assures us that the Gospels tell us what Jesus Christ actually said and did.

They are not myth; even if they were written after the Resurrection with that fuller knowledge which they had when enlightened by the Holy Spirit. All scholars are convinced that Jesus existed, that he performed many miracles, that he taught the kingdom of God, and that he was put to death in the governorship of Pontius Pilate.

Whether or not he was truly the Son of God, of course, is a matter of faith. But just as he challenged people to believe in his message and in his person during his lifetime, so he does today through the reading of the most important part of Scripture to us as Christians, the four Gospels. It is a very good practice to read a portion of the Gospels each day.

Q. Is all the Church's faith contained in the Bible?

A. Not fully. Catholics also believe in the authority of the unwritten Tradition from the apostles. There is a fundamental difference between the Catholic approach to Scripture and that of the Churches of the Reformation. We as Catholics do not believe that the Bible alone is the source of our faith. We believe that the Bible is the Word of God.

But we believe, with Eastern Orthodox Christians, that there is an unwritten source of the Word of God which goes along with the Bible which we call Tradition. Tradition is not just dusty old pictures. Tradition is the faith handed on from the apostles in its entirety, but in unwritten form; in the Church's teaching, in the celebration of the liturgy.

The faith cannot be handed on just in a book, however holy. It needs a living community of faith to hand it on which goes beyond words. Paul himself says in 2 Thessalonians 2:15 that his readers should *'Hold fast to the traditions you have been taught whether by word or by letter'.*

Q. Can you give a good example of the Tradition of Faith?

A. A good example of this Tradition is the doctrine of the Assumption of Mary. Catholics believe that Mary the Mother of God did not suffer the corruption of her body in the grave; but, like her Son Jesus who rose from the dead body and soul, Mary is now in heaven with Jesus body and soul.

We will have to wait the general Resurrection of the Body for that fullness of unity, body and soul. This doctrine of the Assumption is not clearly stated in scripture; but it is part of the living Tradition of the Church, and expresses the deeper meaning of scripture.

This is expressed beautifully by Pope Pius XII in the beginning of the text defining the Assumption in 1950:

> From all eternity and by one and the same decree of predestination the august Mother of God is united in a sublime way with Jesus Christ;

immaculate in her conception, a spotless virgin in her divine motherhood, the noble companion of the divine Redeemer who won a complete triumph over sin and its consequences, she finally obtained as the crowning glory of her privileges to be preserved from the corruption of the tomb and, like her Son before her, to conquer death and to be raised body and soul to the glory of heaven, to shine refulgent as Queen at the right hand of her Son, the immortal King of ages.

Q. What method should I use to read the Bible?

A. There are many methods.

- The Scripture readings at Mass are a very good way of beginning to read the Scriptures for yourself. If you purchase a Missal, you can look at the readings before you go to Mass.
- There are various kinds of daily reading guides, e.g. Bible Alive written in England by Catholic laypeople and priests; and the Bible Reading Fellowship, which is an ecumenical publication.
- One simple way is to read a book of the Bible, a chapter each day. You can start on St. Mark's Gospel, then go on to St. Paul's Letters to the Corinthians.

  Regarding the Old Testament, the books of Samuel and Kings read like an adventure novel. Then perhaps read one of the prophets, not too long, like Hosea.
- The Psalms. These are wonderful prayers. Take a Psalm a day, and in about five months you will have read every one!

In one sense the whole of the Scriptures are in the psalms. (Psalm 118 is too long, 176 verses. Take a couple of sections each day perhaps).

The Rosary is in fact a biblical meditation, in fifteen units.

THE JOYFUL MYSTERIES

FIRST: *THE ANNUNCIATION* Luke 1:26-38

SECOND: *THE VISITATION* Luke 1:39-45

THIRD: *THE BIRTH OF CHRIST* Luke 2:1-20

FOURTH: *PRESENTATION IN THE TEMPLE* Luke 2:22-32

FIFTH: *THE FINDING OF THE CHILD JESUS IN THE TEMPLE*
Luke 2:41-50.

THE SORROWFUL MYSTERIES

FIRST: *THE AGONY IN THE GARDEN* Matthew 26:36-46

SECOND: *THE SCOURGING AT THE PILLAR* Matthew 27:26.

THIRD: *THE CROWNING WITH THORNS* Matthew 27:27-31.

FOURTH: *JESUS CARRIES HIS CROSS* Matthew 22: 32-38

FIFTH: *JESUS IS CRUCIFIED* Matthew 22:39-56

THE GLORIOUS MYSTERIES

FIRST: *THE RESURRECTION* John 20-21.

SECOND: *THE ASCENSION* Acts 1:1-11.

THIRD: *THE DESCENT OF THE HOLY SPIRIT AT
PENTECOST* Acts 2:1-47.

FOURTH: *THE ASSUMPTION OF MARY*
(See Romans 8:31-39. Victory over death).

FIFTH: *THE CORONATION OF MARY AS QUEEN OF HEAVEN*
(See Revelation 12:1-6).

Pope John Paul II, for this new millennium, added another set of five Mysteries to commemorate the wonderful things which happened during the public ministry of Jesus:-

THE MYSTERIES OF LIGHT

FIRST: *THE BAPTISM OF JESUS, Mark 1:9-11*
SECOND: *THE TURNING OF WATER INTO WINE,*
John 2:1-11
THIRD: *JESUS PREACHES THE KINGDOM, HEALS AND CASTS*
OUT DEMONS, Luke 11:20
FOURTH: *THE TRANSFIGURATION, Matthew 17: 1-8*
FIFTH: *THE EUCHARIST, 1 Corinthians 11:23-29*

Each of the fifteen Mysteries is called a 'Decade' (One Our Father, Ten Hail Marys, One Glory Be to the Father).
The repetition of the 'Hail Mary' is a technique to aid concentration while meditating on the Gospel mystery.
Some recite Five Mysteries each day, without rushing but rhythmically, you will find that that takes altogether not much more than 15 minutes.
Pope John Paul II, when he published the Mysteries of Light above, suggested this as a weekly project:-

MONDAY: *THE FIVE JOYFUL MYSTERIES*
TUESDAY: *THE FIVE SORROWFUL MYSTERIES*
WEDNESDAY: *THE FIVE GLORIOUS MYSTERIES*
THURSDAY: *THE FIVE MYSTERIES OF LIGHT*
FRIDAY: *THE FIVE SORROWFUL MYSTERIES*
SATURDAY: *THE FIVE JOYFUL MYSTERIES (Our Lady's Saturday)*
SUNDAY: *THE FIVE GLORIOUS MYSTERIES.*

You can follow the above system when you are used to saying the Rosary. I follow that way myself.

But, at the beginning, a good idea would be to take just one of the mysteries, read the Scripture passage associated with it above, and then just recite that Decade. You will have completed the whole Rosary then in fifteen days! Ask a Catholic who says the Rosary regularly to set you on your way.

Besides these traditional Mysteries of the Rosary there are various additional ones. The Journey Mysteries have been found helpful by many people:

THE JOURNEY MYSTERIES

1. The Baptism of the Lord Jesus in the Jordan. (Mt. 3:13-17)
2. Peter is appointed by the Lord to the Primacy of the Church (Mt.16:13-19. Jn. 21:15-19)
3. The Transfiguration of the Lord Jesus on Mount Tabor (Mt. 17:1-13)
4. The Lord Jesus raises Lazarus from the dead. (John 11:1-54)
5. The Lord gives the Holy Eucharist to the Church at the Last Supper. (Mt. 26:26-30). (Cor. 11:23-34).

GREAT CHRISTIANS
ST. AUGUSTINE OF HIPPO

Born in North Africa (354-430). Brought up a Catholic, but his father who was a pagan delayed his baptism as was usual at that time. For years Augustine lapsed, and followed a heretical religion called the Manichaeans (a kind of 'new age' cult of the day). His mother, St. Monica, prayed continually for him.

Augustine became a famous professor of Rhetoric (the art of public speaking) at Milan, where he came under the influence of the great bishop St. Ambrose. Augustine at that time had a mistress, with whom he had lived for fifteen years, and who bore him a child. But he was beginning to see the stupidity of the Manichaeans, and rejected them. And, one day, when walking in the garden and reading the New Testament, he heard a voice saying 'tolle, lege' ('take up and read'). He turned to Romans 13:13-14.

> Let us conduct ourselves becomingly as in the day, not in revelling and drunkenness, not in debauchery and licentiousness, not in quarreling and jealousy. But let your armour be the Lord Jesus Christ, and make no provision for the flesh, to gratify its desires.

Augustine was converted, and eventually became a bishop and perhaps the greatest Christian thinker of all time after St. Paul. He eventually took charge of his illegitimate son Adeodatus (which means "given by God"), and cared for him. People read his Confessions today as a good spiritual read, in fact as one of the literary classics of all time.

His feast is August 28.

CHAPTER 8
THE HOLY MASS

Q. Why is the Mass the most important religious service in the Catholic Church's life?

A. Because it is the worship which Christ himself left us to do, to save our souls and to unite ourselves with God and with each other.
It is the fulfilment above all of the First Commandment, to worship the Lord our God. We worship God God's way, Jesus' way.

Q. Why is the Mass so sacred?

A. Because we receive the very flesh and blood of Christ as our food. Eighteen hundred years ago, one of the first Christian martyrs, St. Justin the Martyr, *(100-165)*, spoke of the Mass in a way which shows that our faith is the same as his nearly two thousand years after:-

> For we do not receive this food as ordinary bread and as ordinary drink; but just as Jesus Christ our Saviour became flesh through the word of God, and assumed flesh and blood for our salvation, so too we are taught that the food over which the prayer of thanksgiving, the word received from Christ, has been said, the food which nourishes our flesh and blood by assimilation, is the flesh and blood of this Jesus who became flesh.
> The apostles in their memoirs, which are called gospels, recorded that Jesus left them these instructions; he took bread, pronounced

the prayer of thanksgiving, and said: 'Do this in memorial of me. This is my body.' In the same way he took the cup, pronounced the prayer of thanksgiving, and said: 'This is my blood', and shared it among them and no one else. From that time on we have always continued to remind one another of this.

Q. But how can we believe that a piece of bread (or wafer) and a sip of wine can be truly the body and blood of Christ?

A. Through faith, as the Council of Trent states, Session 13, 1551 A.D.:-

To begin with, the Holy Council teaches and openly and straightforwardly confesses that in the Blessed Sacrament of the Holy Eucharist, after the consecration of the bread and wine, our Lord Jesus Christ, true God and man, is truly, really and substantially contained under the appearances of those perceptible realities. For there is no contradiction in the fact that our Saviour always sits at the right hand of the Father in heaven according to his natural way of existing and that, nevertheless, in his substance He is sacramentally present to us in many other places.
We can hardly find words to express this way of existing; but our reason, enlightened through faith, can nevertheless recognise it as possible for God, and we must always believe it unhesitatingly.

For the Council of Trent, therefore, being bread and wine in the Eucharist is one way of being for God.

The normal way we experience God's presence is in the creatures God has created.

They retain their identity.

God is present also in the bread and wine of the Eucharist; but now in such a way that they lose their identity as bread and wine and become the food and drink of Christ for us. We become in a very special way one with him.

Q. Is not this act of faith difficult?

A. Of course; but no more difficult than it was for the first disciples who heard Christ speak in this way:-

> So Jesus said to them, 'Truly, truly I say to you, unless you eat the flesh of the Son of Man and drink his blood, you have no life in you; he who eats my flesh and drinks my blood has eternal life, and I will raise him up on the last day. For my flesh is food indeed, and my blood is drink indeed. He who eats my flesh and drinks my blood abides in me, and I in him. (John 6:53-56, cf. I Corinthians 11:23-27)

Q. Is this not cannibalism, to eat the body and drink the blood of Christ?

A. No, because the presence of Christ is as our food, not in the physical form of a human body. Likewise, the Mass is a sacrifice, but not a repetition of the sufferings of Christ, which ended two thousand years ago on Calvary.

The Mass is a sacrifice of praise, offering the bread and wine in thanksgiving for Christ's once-for-all death on the Cross, to be transformed sacramentally into his body and blood for us now.

Q. Is it a mortal sin to miss Holy Mass on Sundays?

A. Yes, if there is no sufficient reason (e.g. illness, an emergency). The act of the Mass is so solemn that it is surely an insult to God to miss Mass without sufficient reason. It is the Sunday Mass which is an obligation. Again, Justin the Martyr:-

> So on Sunday we all come together. This is the first day, on which God transformed darkness and matter and made the world; the day on which Jesus Christ our Saviour rose from the dead. For on the day before Saturday he was crucified, and on the day after Saturday, that is the Sunday, he appeared to his apostles and disciples and taught them the truths which we have put before you for your consideration.

Q. Why is Holy Mass the 'Sacrament of Love'?

A. Because in the Mass the love of Christ is most fully expressed. Also, from the Mass stems the Church's obligation to help those in need, to give food to those who need it just as Christ feeds us with himself. Justin again:-

> Those of us who are well provided help out any who are in need, and we meet together continually. Over all our offerings we give thanks to the Creator of all through his Son Jesus Christ and the Holy Spirit.

The Catholic Church is the biggest provider of charitable works throughout the world; even bigger than the United States! There are more hospitals and schools in the world run by the Catholic Church than by any other organisation. The Church is committed to putting the Christian concept of love into practice.

Q. Why is it called 'the Mass'?

A. We are not entirely sure. Most likely, it comes from the expression in Latin *Ite, Missa Est,* the deacon saying to the people "Go now, you are dismissed" after the final blessing. *Missa* became 'Mass'. It is a nice thought that *missa est* means also that we are 'dismissed' at the end of Mass to take Christ into his world.

EUCHARIST. Justin uses the word 'Eucharist', the word most frequently used down the centuries. The word means 'thanksgiving', but it also conveys the idea of blessing. The main prayer in the Mass is called the Eucharistic Prayer, because it is a great prayer of thanksgiving.

Q. Why does not the Church allow non-Catholics to receive Holy Communion (the giving of the bread and wine which has now become the body and blood of Christ) to those who wish to receive it?

A. The Church does not normally admit to Communion those who are not in full communion with the Catholic Church. We see Holy Communion as the fruit of unity, not as a means to it. That is in keeping with Justin's point that it is only those who accept the truth of our teachings who can receive Communion. This causes great anguish among some members of other Churches, because they have been baptised, washed in the bath which confers forgiveness of sins and rebirth; but it links up very much with belief in the Real Presence of the Eucharist. (See The Code of Canon Law, London, Collins, 1983, pp.156-157, Canon 844.)

We cannot give Communion to a person who does not believe the Catholic doctrine of the Eucharist, especially the doctrine of the Real Presence as outlined above.

Nevertheless, there are some circumstances where people who are not Catholics may receive Communion from us, e.g. especially in danger of death. This is a complex question, which cannot be fully dealt with here.

Please consult your priest if you wish to discuss the matter further.

GREAT CHRISTIANS
ST. THOMAS AQUINAS
(1225-1274)

We have already met this great saint and intellectual genius in his proofs for God's existence.

Thomas was the son of a rich Italian nobleman, who had ambitions for his son to be the Abbot of one of the large and wealthy monasteries like Monte Cassino. Instead, his son wanted to join a new preaching Order called the Dominicans, who went around from place to place with no money, but preaching the Gospel.

His father tried to make his son a prisoner, even sending into him a woman of easy virtue. But Thomas chased her off with a red hot poker! He joined the Dominicans, and soon became famous for his ability to lecture and dispute.

He travelled all over Europe, walking from one University to another. He wrote perhaps the most famous text-book of theology of all time, called the Summa Theologica.

He was particularly strong on the Catholic doctrine of the Eucharist, countering errors of his own day like that propounded by Berengarius of Tours, who denied the Real Presence of Christ.

He promoted throughout the Church the worship of the Blessed Sacrament.

His feast is January 28.

CHAPTER 9
CONFESSION

Q: Why did Christ institute the Sacrament of Confession, Penance, or Reconciliation?

A: Christ instituted the Sacrament of Reconciliation to make provision within the Church for the forgiveness of sin.

Many people also who feel guilty about what they see is a sin, but which in fact was no sin at all, will also receive assurance from the priest that there was no sin in their case. It can be an occasion of reflecting on where our life is going to, and of spiritual direction.

Q: Can any sin be forgiven?

A: Yes. No sin is so bad that it cannot be forgiven. As we read in the parable of the Prodigal Son (Luke 15:11-32), God our heavenly Father is always ready to welcome us back.

He knows our weakness, but he loves us so much that he is always ready to forgive. Being forgiven in the sacrament of Penance (another name for Confession) gives us that liberation from sin which is so wonderful for us.

Q: Can we be forgiven no matter how many times we have sinned?

A. Yes. There is the story of a man who went to confession and began by saying 'Same old sins, Father'.

The priest replied, 'No problem: same old Absolution'. As the Catechism says:-

When he celebrates the Sacrament of Penance, the priest is fulfilling the ministry of the Good Shepherd who seeks the lost sheep, of the Good Samaritan who binds up wounds, of the Father who awaits the prodigal son and welcomes him on his return, and of the just and impartial judge whose judgement is both just and merciful.

The priest is the sign and the instrument of God's merciful love for the sinner. (1465)

Q. But why do we need to go to a priest for forgiveness of sin? Cannot we receive forgiveness from God alone?

A. Because when we sin, we harm the Church as well as ourselves. We are by our sins out of communion with the Church, and need to receive the forgiveness of the Church in the person of the priest. Going to a priest also helps us to be really sorry for our sins, and to receive the help we need to avoid sin in the future, and to live a fully Christian life.

Q. Do we HAVE to go to Confession?

A. When we have committed a mortal or serious sin. A mortal sin (a deathly sin) is a serious sin which destroys the love of God in us.

God does not cease to love us, and to want us to love him; but we cease to love God, and so the love of God dies in us, by our own fault:-

If you refuse to love, you must remain dead; to hate your brother is to be a murderer, and murderers, as you know, do not have eternal life in them. (1 John 3:15).

The Catechism says:-

> When the will sets itself upon something that is of its nature incompatible with the charity that orients man toward his ultimate end, then the sin is mortal by its very object... whether it contradicts the love of God, such as blasphemy or perjury, or the love of neighbour, such as homicide or adultery... But when the sinner's will is set upon something that of its nature involves a disorder, but is not opposed to the love of God and neighbour, such as thoughtless chatter or immoderate laughter and the like, such sins are venial. *(From Thomas Aquinas, Summa Theologica).* (1855)

Perhaps once a month is a sufficient way to avail of this sacrament unless grave sin requires us to go more often. The Church requires us to go to Confession and Holy Communion at least once per year, during the Lent and Easter season.

Q: How do I know if I have committed a mortal sin?

A: For a sin to be mortal, three conditions must be fulfilled *(cf. CCC 1858-1859)*:

1. The sin must be grave regarding its 'matter'. What is done must be seriously wrong.

2. There must be full knowledge of what we are doing.

3. There must be full consent of the will.

• Grave Matter

What we do needs itself to be seriously wrong in order for it to be a mortal sin. I will list some examples under each of the Ten Commandments:-

I AM THE LORD YOUR GOD. YOU SHALL NOT HAVE STRANGE GODS BEFORE ME.

Satanic worship. Neglect of God... Being so enthusiastic to pursue a goal of our own (a 'created good') that due obligations to God and neighbour are seriously neglected. (Frequent venial sin: neglect of daily prayer).

YOU SHALL NOT TAKE THE NAME OF THE LORD YOUR GOD IN VAIN.

Mocking God and religion. Seriously cursing God. (Not swearing, which is only a venial sin unless great damage or scandal is caused. Also a venial sin: using the name of Jesus lightly).

REMEMBER TO KEEP HOLY THE LORD'S DAY.

Missing Sunday Mass, and on Holydays of Obligation, without adequate reason. Being so 'workaholic' that necessary rest is not taken. Venial sin: not prioritising God and prayer on Sunday.

HONOUR YOUR FATHER AND YOUR MOTHER.

Serious neglect of parents or of dependants. Either refusing to provide for them when such is reasonably possible. Or neglecting to visit them, causing them distress and sadness. Venial sin:

forgetting to pray for them, not showing them sufficient love.

YOU SHALL NOT KILL.

Any unjustified killing. Abortion, euthanasia, suicide: killing in a brawl or to steal. Uncontrolled hatred.
Doing serious harm to oneself by taking hard drugs unprescribed, or by playing a game which involves undue risk to life or limb. (Russian roulette, of course! Suicide surfing. Heavy and persistent drinking.)

YOU SHALL NOT COMMIT ADULTERY.

Adultery itself. 'Trial Marriages'. Homosexual acts. Participation in hard pornography.

YOU SHALL NOT STEAL.

Stealing large sums of money or property. Cheating another person out of a large amount of money by shady dealing.
Persistent laziness at work, taking wages without adequate labour for it.
Not being a good and fair employer; not paying sufficient wages or requiring workers to endure bad conditions of work.

YOU SHALL NOT BEAR FALSE WITNESS AGAINST YOUR NEIGHBOUR.

Destroying a person's reputation deliberately, unless that person has committed a crime or misdemeanour which should be made public. Venial sin: gossip about others.

YOU SHALL NOT COVET YOUR
NEIGHBOUR'S WIFE.

Lustful desire uncontrolled for any kind of sexual
act forbidden under the Sixth Commandment.
Allowing our heart to desire another, or court
danger by cultivating improper friendships with
another's spouse.

YOU SHALL NOT COVET YOUR
NEIGHBOUR'S GOODS.

Uncontrolled desire for wealth (avarice), especially
if such wealth means injustice to another person
or persons.

***However, in order for there to be a mortal
sin:***

• **There must be full knowledge of what we
are doing.**
To take a large sum of money thinking it was a gift,
then finding out that the money had been stolen,
would not be a mortal sin because knowledge was
not there.
But the police might think otherwise!

• **There must be full consent of the will.**
A good example of lack of full consent would be a
person who committed the sin of gluttony
through excessive drinking, but who, because of
their alcohol dependence, may now lack the
freedom to do otherwise. Consent has to be free,
full and deliberate.

All these conditions, all three of them, must be
fulfilled for an act to be a mortal sin.

Clearly, when in doubt, the person to consult is the priest. He will not be like a prosecuting attorney, trying to make a mortal out of a venial sin, more the other way round!

CATHOLICS WHO PRACTISE THE SACRAMENT OF PENANCE REGULARLY KNOW THAT IT IS THE MOST POWERFUL SPIRITUAL HELP THERE IS TO GROW IN GRACE.

Q. Do I have to confess venial (lighter) sins?

A: No. But the Church recommends regular confession of venial sins:-

> *Without being strictly necessary, confession of everyday faults (venial sins) is nevertheless strongly recommended by the Church.*
> *Indeed the regular confession of our venial sins helps us form our conscience, fight against evil tendencies, let ourselves be healed by Christ and progress in the life of the Spirit. By receiving more frequently through this sacrament the gift of the Father's mercy, we are spurred to be merciful as he is merciful.* (CCC 1458)

Q: How do I make a good Confession?

A: Three elements are necessary:-

1. Contrition. I must be truly sorry for my sin, and be determined not to sin again.

2. Confession. I must confess the sin to a priest in the Sacrament if it is a mortal sin.

3. Satisfaction. Again where mortal sin is concerned, reparation must be made of some kind. The priest will give a penance, perhaps a prayer. But, if stealing is involved or a damaged relationship, efforts must be made to repair that damage if at all possible; or restitution where has been serious financial loss. Again, consult the priest.

An old prayer before going to Confession:-

Jesus my Lord, I love You above all things. I repent with my whole heart of having offended You.
Help me never to sin against You again.
Grant that I may love You always; and then do with me what You will. Amen.

P.S. I am particularly grateful for the expert help of my good friend Canon George Woodall, Canon Lawyer and distinguished moral theologian of the diocese of Nottingham, in revising the above Chapter and the following Chapter 10.

GREAT CHRISTIANS
THE CURÉ D'ARS
1786-1859

A priest of the early 19th century France. He was not good at his studies at the seminary, and briefly went off to fight in the war with Napoleon.

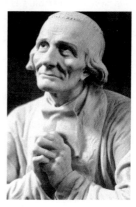

Unlike a previous saint we have mentioned, Ignatius Loyla, he was not a wealthy aristocrat, nor was he a particularly successful soldier!

He returned home after the war, was eventually ordained, and sent by his bishop to the worst parish in the diocese, a small village called Ars where only a handful of people went to Mass. Soon Fr John Vianney gained a reputation worldwide as a confessor, people coming from all over and queuing for hours for his wisdom.

Fr John also founded an orphanage for the poor boys of the area, and the story seems well authenticated that food was miraculously provided.

He died a saint after half a century of ministry in that parish, and having heard many thousands of confessions. He was named by the Pope as the Patron Saint of Parish Priests.

His feast is 4th August.

O FACE
ADORABLE
QUI
REMPLIREZ
LES JUSTES
DE JOIE
PENDANT
L'ÉTERNITÉ
ABAISSEZ
SUR NOS
VOS
REGARDS
DIVINS!

NE
FALLAIT-IL PAS
QUE
LE CHRIST
ENDURÂT
CES
SOUF-
FRANCES
POUR
ENTRER
DANS SA
GLOIRE?

LC 24,26

UNIS
LE
13 JUILLET 18..

DANS L'ÉGLISE
NOTRE-DAME
D'ALENÇON

CHAPTER 10
MARRIAGE AND SEXUALITY

Q. Why does the Church think that marriage is such a 'big deal'? Why get married anyway?

A. It is because the Church believes that God himself is the author of the marriage bond between man and woman. It is not simply a human contract:-

> Then the Lord God said, "It is not good that the man should be alone; I will make him a helper fit for him"... So the Lord God caused a deep sleep to fall upon the man, and while he slept took one of his ribs and closed up its place with flesh; and the rib which the Lord God had taken from the man he made into a woman and brought her to the man.
> Then the man said, "This at last is bone of my bones and flesh of my flesh; she shall be called Woman, because she was taken out of Man."
> Therefore a man leaves his father and his mother and cleaves to his wife, and they become one flesh. (Genesis 2:18-25)

Q. But surely all this about taking woman from the 'rib' of the man is sheer myth?

A. Yes, of course. We must begin by saying that the story of the 'rib' need not be taken literally.
As we have seen before, Pope Pius XII, in his encyclical *Humani Generis* ('Of the Human Race') made it clear that it was not incompatible with Catholic theology to hold that the human being evolved from lower animals (Darwin's apes);

provided that it was maintained that the soul was created in each individual human being, even if the father or mother were pre-hominoids.

The story uses figurative language here. The 'rib' is a way in which the story-teller emphasises the fact that the woman is of the same flesh as the man, one with him in body even before marriage, and of equal dignity with him.

The central point of the story is that man and woman in marriage become 'one flesh'. The word 'flesh' here does not mean just a physical union, although that of course is involved.

It is a union of two persons to become one in heart and mind as well as in body. Thus the union is permanent, for life, and exclusive. Otherwise its unity is destroyed by another alien party coming in to destroy that union.

Q. But does not the Bible teach that sex is sinful? Was not that the 'Original Sin', Adam and Eve having sex together against God's will?

A. Not at all. The story about the man 'cleaving' to his wife so that the two become one flesh is prior to the story of the Fall in Genesis 3.

The sexual act is for the Scriptures essentially good and a great and legitimate pleasure. God is pleased too for the couple involved! In fact, it is a pleasure even after the Fall of Adam and Eve:-

> Now Adam had intercourse with Eve his wife, and she conceived and bore Cain, saying, "I have gotten a man with the help of the LORD." (Gen 4:1)

The sin of our first parents was not sexual, it was the sin of pride, of refusing to obey the will of God.

Q. Is not the Church prudish about sex, being ashamed of nudity and so on?

A. The shame we feel at our nakedness is the result of sin. We are implicitly threatened by the thought that, if we are naked, our own or the other peoples' sexual feelings will be inordinately stimulated by looking at us.

Or we will feel violated by being an object of sexual stimulation when we wish it not to be so.

The solution is not brazen nudity, acting as if concupiscence were not there.

The answer lies again in the wisdom of tradition, that we should be modest, protecting oneself and others against concupiscence by discretion; keeping the revelation of nudity either within the intimacy of marriage and the family, same-sex living situations, or for professional requirements (medical, artistic.).

The Catechism says:-

> Purity requires modesty, an integral part of temperance. Modesty protects the intimate centre of the person. It means refusing to unveil what should remain hidden.
> It is ordered to chastity to whose sensitivity it bears witness. It guides how one looks at others and behaves toward them in conformity with the dignity of persons and their solidarity. (2521)

Q. Why is the Catholic Church against divorce?

A. Because this is the way Jesus argues when questioned about his teaching on marriage by the Pharisees:-

> And Pharisees came up to him and tested him by asking, "Is it lawful to divorce one's wife for any cause?"
> He answered, "Have you not read that he who made them from the beginning made them male and female, and said, 'For this reason a man shall leave his father and mother and be joined to his wife, and the two shall become one flesh'?
> So they are no longer two but one flesh. What therefore God has joined together, let not man put asunder." (Matthew 19:3-6)

For this reason, the Church does not allow the remarriage of divorced couples, while allowing separation under certain circumstances.

Q. Why, then, does the Church declare annulments? Is this not the same?

A. No. The Catholic Church does allow annulment of marriages, where it is clear that there was some impediment invalidating that marriage.

The point is that the marriage was essentially defective from the start.

That is in no way the same as breaking a marriage bond where the marriage has been perfectly valid. If you have a query in this regard, do not hesitate to see your priest to discuss it further.

As with many aspects of law, these issues can be complicated, and you will need to talk with an expert.

Q. Why does the Church call marriage a 'sacrament'?:

A. Because a sacramental marriage is a union blessed by Christ himself. It is a great means of grace and spiritual help to the couple. The couple 'give' each other the sacrament, to be for each other a means of grace until their lives end. See Ephesians 5:21-33.

Marriage being a sacrament means especially that God helps each married couple to be faithful to God, to each other, and to their vows.

Q. Why, then, is the Church against contraception?

A. I wondered how long it would be before we got round to that!

> The Church, which "is on the side of life" teaches that "each and every marriage act must remain open to the transmission of life." "This particular doctrine, expounded on numerous occasions by the Magisterium, is based on the inseparable connection, established by God, which man on his own initiative may not break, between the unitive significance and the procreative significance which are both inherent to the marriage act." (CCC 2866)

The Church, as is well known, allows the use of the 'safe period', which does not positively obstruct conception, but which does allow the natural rhythms to be used in timing the act of intercourse, to seek to avoid a child where there are good reasons for such an intention.

Everyone realises the difficulty of this teaching. It is worth looking again at the previous chapter on Mortal Sin. In some cases, one spouse may be under such pressure from the other to use contraception that the degree of the former spouse's responsibility may be reduced. This is a matter to talk over with a priest or with a marriage counsellor, faithful to the Church's teaching.

Q. Why, then, is the Church against all sex which is outside of marriage?

A. Because all sex outside of marriage falls short of the norm of sexuality, ordained by the Creator from the beginning, that it should be unitive and procreative within marriage.

The very pleasure of the sexual act is ordained by the Creator to make the beginning of a family an act of joy and love of the couple. It is perverse to make it a pleasure for itself alone.

This means that homosexual unions (sometimes called homosexual marriages), that is same-sex couples living together, are wrong and that intimate homosexual acts are against God's law. This is because they are neither truly complementary nor open to procreation.

Of course, this does not mean that the Church does not encourage same-sex friendships, which are a great gift to us all. It is the sexual dimension which is not morally acceptable.

For the same reason, the Church has named deliberate masturbation, homosexual acts, acts of bestiality, acts of paedophilia, as always in themselves wrong, as with 'trial marriages' and 'living together without marriage'.

All these activities essentially lack the fullness of union of love and life which we find from the beginning as God's will regarding marriage.

For this reason, the Church calls these acts 'morally wrong', that is wrong by their very nature *per se*, and can never be right.

Q. Surely chastity is a waste of time?

A. Look back at the Chapter on Confession. There must always be the effort to gain purity of mind and heart, which may result in a long battle with our disordered nature.

We will win in the end! You will find a priest in the confessional most helpful here:-

> *Chastity includes an apprenticeship in self-mastery which is a training in human freedom. The alternative is clear: either man governs his passions and finds peace, or he lets himself be dominated by them and becomes unhappy.*
> *Man's dignity therefore requires him to act out of conscious and free choice, as moved and drawn in a personal way from within, and not by blind impulses in himself or by mere external constraint.*
> *Man gains such dignity when, ridding himself of all slavery to the passions, he presses forward to his goal by freely choosing what is good and, by his diligence and skill, effectively secures for himself the means suited to this end.* (CCC 2339)

GREAT CHRISTIANS
MARGARET OF CORTONA
(1297 A.D.)

Margaret was born in Tuscany, Italy. Her mother died when she was young, and her step-mother treated her without affection.

Margaret soon fell in love with a dashing young cavalier, by whom she had a child. Unfortunately, her lover was assassinated, and his dog returned to her care without his master, Margaret did penance for her sins, devoting her life to serving the poor, nursing them herself.

She was also fearless in denouncing her own bishop, who was too fond of going to war to settle his quarrels. Eventually, he died in battle.

On the day of her death she was publicly proclaimed as a saint by the people, but she was not formally declared a saint by the Church until 1728.

Her feast is 22nd February.

CHAPTER 11
MY VOCATION

Q. Are all equally members of the body of Christ?

A. Absolutely:-

> *In virtue of their rebirth in Christ there exists among all the Christian faithful a true equality with regard to dignity and the activity whereby all cooperate in the building up of the Body of Christ in accord with each one's own condition and function.* **(872)**

The Church baptises infants. The tiniest and most vulnerable of us can be fully Catholics. Physical, mental handicap, being a prisoner, outcasts of society, none of this constitutes a barrier to membership of the Church.

One of the complaints his contemporaries had about Jesus was *(Luke 15:2)* *"This fellow welcomes sinners and eats with them."*

A beggar with smelly clothes who is a Catholic will receive Communion. The local Mayor who is not a Catholic will not be invited. The Church is the most inclusive club in the world, and yet does have rules of membership.

Rich, poor, beggar, thief, millionaires, unemployed, all are welcome in the Church, even though they may be required to make some tough decisions regarding their lives!

Q. Everyone, therefore, has a vocation?

A. Most certainly:-

> Lay believers are in the front line of Church life; for them the Church is the animating principle of human society. Therefore, they in particular ought to have an ever-clearer consciousness not only of belonging to the Church, but of being the Church, that is to say, the community of the faithful on earth under the leadership of the Pope, the common Head, and of the bishops in communion with him. They are the Church. (CCC 899)

Every lay person, therefore, should be conscious of having a vocation to live the Gospel in his or her situation, wherever or whatever it might be.

Q. What of parents of children?

A. They have a very special vocation. Every father and mother of a family has a special vocation to bring up their children. That is some mission in life, especially today! Each family is in a sense to be a reflection of the Holy Family of Jesus, Mary, and Joseph. In that Holy Family, Jesus the Son of God 'increased in wisdom, in stature, and in favour with God and everyone':-

> In a very special way, parents share in the office of sanctifying by leading a conjugal life in the Christian spirit and by seeing to the Christian education of their children. (902)

This will involve:-

- Teaching your children to pray and taking them to Holy Mass.
- Sharing your own knowledge of your faith with them.
- Sending them to a Catholic school where this is possible.
- Making sure that they prepare for their First Holy Communion and encouraging them to prepare for Confirmation.
- Above all, being an example of Christian living.

The fact that you will not be a perfect example will not be in itself a difficulty. None of us are perfect! Even Peter, the first leader of the Church after Christ, denied Jesus three times when under pressure *(Matthew 26:69-75)*. Be an example by taking them to Confession.

Q. What of single people?

A. They have a vocation also. People are free not to marry as well as to marry. Many make a positive decision not to marry, e.g. to serve the Church, to look after aged parents or handicapped relatives. Then widows, victims of broken marriages, all can find a purpose within the community of the Church and its life; also to be as active as possible within the local secular community.

But even when a person has no ability or inclination to be active, we can all pray. Sometimes, one who prays and can do nothing else can possibly be the most valuable person in the Church:-

On the contrary, the members of the body that seem to be weaker are indispensable,

*and those members of the body that we think
less honourable we clothe with greater
honour, and our less respectable members are
treated with greater respect; whereas our
more respectable members do not need this.
But God has so arranged the body, giving the
greater honour to the inferior members, that
there may be no dissension within the body,
but the members may have the same care for
one another.* (1 Corinthians 12:12-25)

Q. What of being a priest?

A. The priest has a very special ministry within the
Church. The priest is ordained in a sacramental
rite, where the bishop lays his hands on him
invoking the power of the Holy Spirit:-

*In the ecclesial service of the ordained
minister, it is Christ himself who is present to
his Church as Head of his Body, Shepherd of
his flock, High Priest of the redemptive
sacrifice, Teacher of Truth. This is what the
Church means by saying that the priest, by
virtue of the sacrament of Holy Orders, acts in
persona Christi Capitis ('in the person of
Christ as Head').* (CCC 1548)

Q. The priest, then, has to be a very holy person?

A. Yes, he is called to be. But he is human also:-

*This presence of Christ in the minister is not to
be understood as if the latter were preserved
from all human weaknesses, the spirit
of domination, error, even sin. The power of
the Holy Spirit does not guarantee all acts*

of ministers in the same way. While this guarantee extends to the sacraments, so that even the minister's sin cannot impede the fruit of grace, in many other acts the minister leaves human traces that are not always signs of fidelity to the Gospel and consequently can harm the apostolic fruitfulness of the Church. (CCC 1550)

Q. Why cannot priests marry?

A. This is a rule which applies to all Catholics in the Western discipline; but even here, occasionally the Church will permit a married man to exercise his priesthood. But usually, the priest is celibate, and this for a particular reason:-

Celibacy is in very many ways appropriate to the priesthood. For the whole mission of a priest is a dedication to the service of the new humanity, which Christ who triumphed over death brings into being in the world by his Spirit, and which draws its origin 'not of blood nor of the will of the flesh nor of the will of man, but of God'. (John 1:13)
Through virginity or celibacy preserved for the sake of the kingdom of heaven, priests are consecrated to Christ in a new and exalted manner, and more easily cleave to him with singleness of heart; in him and through him they devote themselves with greater freedom to the service of God and people; they are more untrammelled in serving his kingdom and his work of heavenly regeneration; and thus they are more equipped to accept a wider fatherhood in Christ. (Vatican II, Decree on Priestly Ministry and Life).

Q. Why can only men be ordained priest?

A. This is because Christ only ordained men to be his apostles, and the Church has not the power to change this rule of Christ. The priest acts as the head of the Body of Christ, in the Holy Mass, in Confession, and as Pastor in the parish; thus it is appropriate that the priest, like Christ, should be male.

Q. What is the most important vocation of all?

A. The Church recommends especially those monks and nuns who follow a life of contemplative prayer. Like Mary, the sister of Martha, who was rebuked for not helping in the kitchen rather than being with Jesus (Luke 10:38), they have 'chosen the better part', the life of prayer.

There are hundreds of thousands of monks, nuns, priests and sisters in religious congregations all over the world. They witness to the love of Christ by their consecration to poverty (no property of their own) chastity and obedience to their community way of life. They are an immense resource of spirituality in the Church.

But every life lived in faith is equally precious. God is served by each one of us living in kindness and faith whatever we do, wherever we are.

Each one of us is called to live his or her unique vocation as a Catholic Christian as we are, how we are, where we are. It's the heart that counts!

GREAT CHRISTIANS
ST. THÉRÈSE OF LISIEUX
1873-1897

A popular saint of the twentieth century. Thérèse lost her mother at an early age, and loved her widowed father very much.

Early in life, she wanted to enter a strict Carmelite convent. She even went to the Pope to ask his favour! She did enter very young, still very much a teenager.

Her father became ill, which was a great cross for her. She herself became sick, and died in her early twenties. What was special about her life?

She would herself say 'nothing, except love', That was her supreme vocation. She wrote an autobiography entitled Story of a Soul, which became a best seller.

After her death, millions went on pilgrimage to Lisieux. Among them, the child Edith Piaf, who became a great singer. Edith had literally been picked up off the street by prostitutes, after having been abandoned. She was blind. The prostitutes took her to Lisieux, and Edith was cured.

She always had a great devotion to Thérèse, always burning a candle in a Catholic Church before she performed on stage.

St. Therese of Lisieux's feast is 1st October.

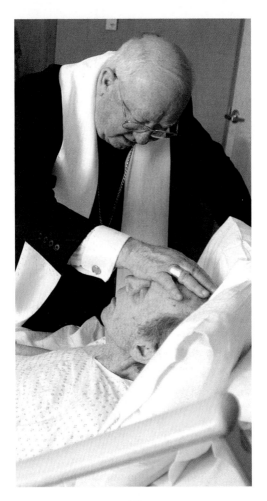

CHAPTER 12
FINAL JOURNEY

Q. Why does God allow sickness and pain?

A. Not generally as a result of personal sin. Jesus Christ was once asked concerning a man who was blind from birth:

> 'Rabbi, who sinned, this man or his parents...?' Jesus replied 'Neither he nor his parents sinned, he was born blind so that the works of God might be displayed in him' (John 9:1-3).

Thomas Aquinas argued that the only ultimate answer to suffering and to evil is that God allows it only in order to bring out something better.
This means that we have to look at the world in terms of its final plan. Paul was able to see all his sufferings as part of that plan. Julian of Norwich said, 'All things will be well; and all manner of things will be well'.

Q. But has Original Sin nothing at all to do with sickness and suffering?

A. The Church sees both suffering and death in the general human condition as the consequence of Original Sin. This is one of the most difficult doctrines to understand. Is sickness, and death, only a natural process which would take place with or without sin? Perhaps death would have happened, in the sense of the transformation of our bodies into the glorious resurrection body. And at least we would have avoided the amount of sickness, much of which does come from the human misuse of the environment.

Q. What special help does the Church give to those who are sick?

A. The Church gives the Sacrament of the Anointing of the Sick. St. James 5:14-15 refers to the anointing of the sick at the beginning of the Church's history.

Only a priest can give this Sacrament, because, like the Holy Mass and the Sacrament of Confession, the priest represents Christ as the Head of the Church giving his special care in this way:-

> By celebrating this sacrament the Church, in the communion of saints, intercedes for the benefit of the sick person, and he, for his part, though the grace of this sacrament, contributes to the sanctification of the Church and to the good of all men for whom the Church suffers and offers herself through Christ to God the Father. (CCC 1522)

Q. Who can receive this Sacrament?

A. Anyone who is seriously ill, not necessarily one who is dying. If given to one seriously ill, the Sacrament may well contribute to that person's healing.

Wonderful things have happened through this Sacrament, even miracles of healing.

But for that we must trust to God's grace. In any case, great spiritual help for a sick person is always available through the Anointing of the Sick.

Q. How does this Sacrament help one who is dying?

A. Together with the Sacrament of Reconciliation, Holy Communion, and the Pope's special Apostolic Blessing for those who are dying, one who is terminally sick is prepared for that final and most important journey of all:-

> *A preparation for the final journey. If the sacrament of anointing the sick is given to all who suffer from serious illness and infirmity, even more rightly is it given to those at the point of departing this life; so it is also called sacramentum exeuntium (the sacrament of those departing).*
>
> *The Anointing of the Sick completes our conformity to the death and Resurrection of Christ, just as Baptism began it. It completes the holy anointings that mark the whole Christian life: that of Baptism which sealed the new life in us, and that of Confirmation which strengthened us for the combat of this life. This last anointing fortifies the end of our earthly life like a solid rampart for the final struggles before entering the Father's house.* (CCC 1523)

N.B. It is most important for a person who is seriously sick, even more for one who is dying, to call a priest. Make sure that relatives and those close to you are aware of this, and make it clear that in the case of an emergency, you wish to see a Catholic priest immediately. Put your wishes in writing if necessary. Hospitals and emergency services will not always do this unless requested.

Q. Do we have to talk about death?

A. This is a taboo subject in the modern secular world. We naturally recoil from it. We once more quote from Vatican II's Church in the Modern World:

> It is in regard to death that man's condition is most shrouded in doubt. Man is tormented not only by pain and by the gradual breaking-up of his body but also, and even more, by the dread of forever ceasing to be.
> But a deep instinct leads him rightly to shrink from and to reject the utter ruin and total loss of his personality. Because he bears in himself the seed of eternity, which cannot be reduced to mere matter, he rebels against death. All the aids made available by technology, however useful they may be, cannot set his anguished mind at rest. They may prolong his life-span; but this does not satisfy his heartfelt longing, one that can never be stifled, for a life to come. (GS 18)

Q. What should be the Christian approach to death?

A. Positive, because we know that, as Christ said, he has gone to prepare a place for us. St. Paul, the great Christian apostle, seems to have achieved almost indifference whether he lives or dies:-

> For to me, living is Christ and dying is gain. If I am to live in the flesh, that means fruitful labour for me; and I do not know which I prefer. I am hard pressed between the two: my desire is to depart and be with Christ, for

that is far better; but to remain in the flesh is more necessary for you. Since I am convinced of this, I know that I will remain and continue with all of you for your progress and joy in faith, so that I may share abundantly in your boasting in Christ Jesus when I come to you again. (Philippians 1:21-26).

Q. Is it not natural to be frightened of death?

A. Of course. One famous man once said that he was not frightened of death, but frightened of dying. A celebrated comedian said that he was not frightened of death, but just had no wish to be there when it happened!
Any journey into the unknown is fearful. But we know that the vision of God awaits us, with the help of God and his Church, as we prepare to meet him face to face.

Q. Can it ever be right to terminate life deliberately in order to avoid suffering?

A. No. "Thou shalt not kill" refers to killing any innocent person, including oneself in suicide or euthanasia.

> *Those whose lives are diminished or weakened deserve special respect. Sick or handicapped persons should be helped to lead lives as normal as possible.* (CCC 2276)
> *Whatever its motives and means, direct euthanasia consists in putting an end to the lives of handicapped, sick or dying persons. It is morally unacceptable.* (CCC 2277)

However,

Discontinuing medical procedures that are burdensome, dangerous, extraordinary, or disproportionate to the expected outcome can be legitimate; it is the refusal of "over-zealous" treatment. Here one does not will to cause death; one's inability to impede it is merely accepted. The decisions should be made by the patient if he is competent and able or, if not, by those legally entitled to act for the patient, whose reasonable will and legitimate interests must always be respected. (CCC 2278)

Q. But how do we know that we will go to heaven, not to the other place?

A. We will not go to hell unless we deliberately decide against God in unforgiven mortal sin. May God prevent us doing that, and enable us to finally repent of all our sins before death. But, for those of us who are imperfect, there may be a time of Purgatory for us as a preparation for heaven:-

All who die in God's grace and friendship, but still imperfectly purified, are indeed assured of their eternal salvation; but after death they undergo purification, to achieve the holiness necessary to enter the joy of heaven. (CCC 1030)

Q. Will we all be judged at the Last Day when Christ returns in glory?

A. Yes. We do not know when that will be. It will rather be 'like a thief in the night'
(1 Thessalonians 5:2).

For man , this consummation will be the final realisation of the unity of the human race, which God willed from creation and of which the pilgrim Church has been "in the nature of sacrament." Those who are united with Christ will form the community of the redeemed, "the holy city" of God, "the Bride, the wife of the Lamb." She will not be wounded any longer by sin, stains, self-love, that destroy or wound the earthly community.

The beatific vision, in which God opens himself in an inexhaustible way to the elect, will be the ever-flowing well-spring of happiness, peace, and mutual communion. (CCC 1045)

AMEN: COME, LORD JESUS. MAY THE GRACE OF THE LORD JESUS BE WITH YOU ALL. AMEN.

(Revelation 22:20-21)

GREAT CHRISTIANS

FILL IN YOUR OWN NAME

....

Your chances of being a canonised saint are about the same as winning the lottery! But the New Testament calls all Christians 'saints'. That is because all of us are called to holiness, and are in the Communion of Saints.

Those millions who have gone to heaven are watching us now, that 'great crowd of witnesses' *(Hebrews 12:1)* are cheering us on and praying for us.

We all have our own crosses to bear and our glory to win. Only God knows what acts of Christian heroism YOU will be called to and will respond to.

'Let us not lose sight of Jesus, who leads us in our faith and brings it to perfection.' *(Hebrews 12:2)*

AMEN!

Some useful prayers

THE SIGN OF THE CROSS

In the name of the Father
and of the Son
and of the Holy Spirit.
Amen.

We make the Sign of the Cross upon ourselves to remember and celebrate our Baptism, by which we became adopted as children of God, heirs of heaven, and received the divine life into our deepest self.

THE LORD'S PRAYER

Our Father, who art in heaven, hallowed be
thy name.
Thy kingdom come.
Thy will be done on earth as it is in heaven.
Give us this day our daily bread,
and forgive us our trespasses,
as we forgive those who trespass against us.
And lead us not into temptation,
but deliver us from evil,
Amen.

THE HAIL MARY

Hail, Mary full of grace,
the Lord is with thee:
blessed art thou you amongst women,
and blessed is the fruit of thy womb, Jesus.
Holy Mary, Mother of God,
pray for us sinners,
now, and at the hour of our death,
Amen.

THE NICENE CREED

We believe in one God,
the Father, the Almighty,
maker of heaven and earth,
of all that is, seen and unseen.
We believe in one Lord Jesus Christ,
the only Son of God,
Eternally begotton of the Father,
God from God, Light from Light,
true God from true God,
begotten, not made,
of one Being with the Father.
Through Him all things were made.
For us men and for our salvation
he came down from heaven:
(We bow in praying the next three lines)
by the power of the Holy Spirit
he became incarnate from the Virgin Mary,
and was made man.
For our sake he was crucified under Pontius
Pilate; he suffered death and was buried.
On the third day he rose again
in accordance with the Scriptures;

he ascended into heaven and is seated at the right hand of the Father.
He will come again in glory to judge the living and the dead,and his kingdom will have no end.
We believe in the Holy Spirit, the Lord, the giver of life, who proceeds from the Father and the Son.
With the Father and the Son he is worshipped and glorified.
He has spoken through the Prophets.
We believe in one holy Catholic and apostolic Church.
We acknowledge one baptism for the forgiveness of sins.
We look for the resurrection of the dead, and the life of the world to come. Amen.

(Based on the Creed of the Council of
  Nicaea. 325)

THE DOXOLOGY

Glory be to the Father, and to the Son, and to the Holy Spirit. (We bow saying this line)
As it was in the beginning, is now and ever shall be, world without end. Amen.

(The reason we bow in this prayer is to honour and worship the one true God, the Blessed Trinity, whose very life we share in and through our Baptism).

FOR THE DAY AHEAD

O God, grant to us those things which
will help us live this day with joy and
generosity:
Give us: A sense of proportion, that we may
see what is important, and what is not;
that we may not be irritated by things which
do not matter.
Give us: A sense of humour, that we may
learn to laugh, and especially to laugh at
ourselves, and not to take ourselves too
seriously.
Give us: A continual awareness of your
presence; that we may do nothing which it
would grieve you to see and say nothing
which it would hurt you to hear.
Give us: Above all else,
the gift of your own Divine Life;
Send us your Holy Spirit from your Son
Jesus Christ, so that we will have the
power of your love within us
to do all the good things with which this
day will challenge us.
May we not rely on our own poor resources
but on the unlimited power of your love which
you freely give us in your Holy Spirit.
Amen.

THE HOLY CHURCH

Lord our God,
preserve in your peace the Holy Catholic
Church throughout the world,
especially in those places where living the
faith is made hard by unjust laws.
Bless our Holy Father the Pope, the
Servant of the Servants of God.
Strengthen him in his mission of preserving
the unity and truth of your Church.
Give to us a deeper sense of your presence
in the Sacraments, in prayer, in silence, in nature.
Help us to find you in serving the poor,
the sad, the weary and those without hope.
Keep your Church steady in your way,
united in love, tolerance, patience and
good humour. Amen.

A PRAYER IN DOUBT

Lord, I have often thought, supposing you
are not there at all?
Could it be true, what many say, that you
do not exist?
Not really, but I cannot help thinking so
sometimes.
And yet, at the risk of speaking into darkness,
I ask you to give me a tiny grain of faith.
Reach out to me so that I may find you as
I seek for you.
I make mine the prayer of the man in the
Gospel: "Lord, I believe, help my unbelief."
Amen (Mk. 9:25)

WHEN LONELY

*"Can a women forget the baby at her
breast, feel no pity for the child she has
borne? Even if these were to forget,
I shall never forget you.
Look, I have engraved you on the palms of
my hands."* (ISAIAH 49: 15-16)

WHEN AFRAID

*"The word of Yahweh came to me saying:
'Before I formed you in the womb I knew
you; before you came to birth I consecrated you;
...Do not be afraid of confronting
them, for I am with you to rescue you,
Yahweh declares."* (Jeremiah 1:4, 5, 8.)

WHEN UNCERTAIN

*"You have already been told what is right
and what Yahweh wants of you.
Only this: to act justly, to love mercy,
to walk humbly with your God."*
(MICAH 6:8)

THE TEN COMMANDMENTS

1. I am the Lord your God, you shall not have strange gods before me.
2. You shall not take the name of the Lord your God in vain.
3. Remember to keep holy the Sabbath Day.
4. Honour your father and your mother.
5. You shall do no murder.
6. You shall not commit adultery.
7. You shall not steal.
8. You shall not bear false witness against your neighbour.
9. You shall not covet your neighbour's wife.
10. You shall not covet your neighbour's goods.

(Based on Exodus 20: 1-17)

THE SIX PRECEPTS OF THE CHURCH

1. To keep Sundays and Holydays of Obligation holy, by attending Holy Mass and by resting from unnecessary work.
2. To keep the days of Fasting and Abstinence appointed by the Church. To abstain from meat, or another food, or do a special act of kindness on Friday, in memory of the Lord Jesus' death for us on that day.
3. To go to confession when you are conscious of a serious sin.
4. To receive Holy Communion at least once a year - at Eastertide or thereabouts.
5. To help the life and mission of the Church by making a regular donation when you can.
6. Not to marry a close relative.

THE SEVEN CORPORAL WORKS OF MERCY

1. To feed the hungry.
2. To give drink to the thirsty.
3. To clothe the naked.
4. To give shelter to the homeless.
5. To visit the sick.
6. To visit the imprisoned.
7. To bury the dead.

THE SEVEN SPIRITUAL WORKS OF MERCY

1. To advise those in doubt.
2. To instruct those in ignorance.
3. To correct sinners.
4. To comfort those in sorrow.
5. To forgive those who offend us.
6. To bear wrongs with patience.
7. To pray for the living and the dead.

THE GREAT COMMANDMENT

The Lord Jesus teaches:
"This is the first:
Hear, O Israel, the Lord our God, the Lord
is one, you must love the Lord your God
with all your heart, with all your soul, with
all your might and with all your strength.
"This is the second:
You must love your neighbour as yourself.
There is no commandment greater than
these." (Mark 12: 29-31)

THE LAST SUPPER WAS
THE FIRST MASS

Saint Paul says: *"For the tradition I received from the Lord and also handed on to you is: that on the night he was betrayed, the Lord Jesus took some bread, and after he had given thanks, he broke it, and said, 'This is my body which is for you; do this in remembrance of me.'*

And in the same way with the cup after supper saying, 'This cup is the new covenant in my blood. Whenever you drink it, do this as a memorial of me." (1 Cor. 11: 23-25)

IN THE EVENING

The Lord Jesus invites us:
"Come to me all you who labour and are overburdened, and I will give you rest. Shoulder my yoke and learn of me, for I am gentle and humble in heart, and you will find rest for your souls. Yes, my yoke is easy and my burden light." (Matthew 11: 28-30)

Lord it is late and I am tired and far from home. I am lonely and among strangers. The day that is past was the usual mixture; I am not proud of everything I did or said. I have not always been aware of myself, of why I did the things I did or adopted certain attitudes.

Stay with me to calm me down and see me
safely asleep.
Bless me with a restful night.
Awaken me to a new day with a glad heart
and a light step;
putting behind me my yesterday,
and resolved to live the next at peace with
you and all your creation.
For I know your Holy Spirit is with me
and his power is sufficient for all good things
if I but let him work in me.
Amen.

STRIVING FOR PERFECTION

THE BEATITUDES

The Lord Jesus says:
"Blessed are the poor in spirit:
the kingdom of Heaven is theirs.
Blessed are the gentle:
they shall inherit the earth.
Blessed are those who mourn:
they shall be comforted.
Blessed are those who hunger and thirst
for what is right:
they shall have their fill.
Blessed are the merciful:
they shall have mercy shown them.
Blessed are the pure in heart:
they shall see God.
Blessed are the peacemakers:
they shall be known as the children of God.
Blessed are those who are persecuted
because they do right:
the kingdom of Heaven is theirs.

Blessed are you when people abuse you and persecute you
and speak evil and false words against you because you believe in me:
rejoice and be glad, for your reward will be great in heaven."
(Matthew 5: 1-12)

PRAYER OF ST. IGNATIUS OF LOYOLA

Teach us, good Lord
To serve You as You deserve
To give and not to count the cost
To fight and not to heed the wounds
To toil and not to seek for rest
To labour and not to ask for any reward
Saving that of knowing that we do Your will.
Through Jesus Christ our Lord.
Amen.

A PRAYER LAST THING AT NIGHT

Visit this house, we pray you, Lord
drive far away all the snares of the enemy
May your holy angels stay here and guard us
in peace and let your blessing be always
upon us. Through Christ our Lord. Amen.

First published Feb 1999
Second Edition June 1999
Third Edition July 2009

Nihil Obstat and Imprimatur:
Right Rev Terence Brain,
Bishop of Salford, 30 July 2009

The *Imprimatur* is a declaration that a book or
pamphlet is considered to be free from doctrinal or moral
error. It is not implied that those who have granted the
Imprimatur agree with the contents,
opinions or statements expressed

ISBN 978-1-904657-49-1

Published by Gabriel Communications Ltd, 4th Floor
Landmark House, Station Road, Cheadle Hulme,
Cheshire SK8 7JH.
Tel. 0161 488 1749 Fax. 0161 488 1701
Design, layout and typography by Joe Kelly
and Catherine Adams
Printed by Buxton Press Limited, Palace Road, Buxton,
Derbyshire SK17 6AE